MAKE 'EM BEG TO PUBLISH YOUR BOOK

How to Reach a Larger Audience & Make a Full-Time Income in the Extremely Overcrowded World of Personal Development

BY DR. ANGELA E. LAURIA

Difference Press

McLean, Virginia USA

Published 2017

ISBN: 978-1-68309-209-4

DISCLAIMER

Cover Design: Ann Alger

Editing: Anna Paradox

Cover photo courtesy of Monica True

Author's photo courtesy of Danielle Cohen

Back cover author photo courtesy of Jenn Reid

To My Mom

For Never Saying No to Buying Me a Book

TABLE OF CONTENTS

INTRODUCTION

I wrote this book while travelling with my family on a river-boat cruise down the Danube from Vienna to Belgrade. I have no doubt the river and the towns along it changed me and some of this book on the journey, as the two – the vacation and the book – are paired like twins in my mind.

I had no idea I would be writing a book while I was on vacation. I took my laptop, yes, and this book had been dancing in my mind for seven months, but I guess I needed the river to coax it out of me.

I met with Nora Ganescu, one of my favorite author-clients, twice along the Danube. First, when I was in Vienna at the start of the trip and then on the third day, in her hometown of Bratislava. Nora had just gotten a print copy of her first book, *The CEO's Playbook* and I couldn't wait to have a copy signed for myself. We spent a day together meandering around the Belvedere Museum looking at Klimt paintings and talking about books and business.

It was that conversation at the Belvedere that sparked the thought "I might write my book here." But how could I do it without skipping the city tours, alienating my family, and missing the opportunity to relax?

The answer, I learned on day two, lay in the river. It was the answer for me and it's the answer for you if you want to do something impossible with your book and your business – something as impossible as writing a powerful, life-changing book, while on vacation with your family and not missing a second of it.

A tour guide in Vienna accidentally gave me the secret. We were returning from a tour of Schönbrunn Palace on a large coach and we crossed a river that wasn't the Danube. The tour guide piped up.

"This river we are crossing," she said, "is called 'The Little Danube.' In the 19th century, the river you are travelling on was not like the river you see today. There were many *Danubes*. And there was much fighting in the city of Vienna about which should be the main Danube."

"It was not until 1870 when the Habsburgs got around to regulating the river system that would become *the* Danube."

"Regulation went on for two decades," she continued, "and during this time many adjustments were made. Once the river was picked, engineers in the city had to direct the water to this main river. They had to make it wider but they also had to build barrier islands to make sure the power of the river did not flood the city. Most of all, they wanted to straighten the river to make trade easier and make it possible for more ships to travel down the Danube reducing the cost of goods and making the cities in the Habsburg Empire along the Danube stronger."

River regulation! I had never heard of this! Have you? But it makes *perfect* sense and it was the key to the long reign of the Habsburgs. They knew the strength and power of directing the flow of a river.

Maria Theresa, the only female ruler of the

Habsburg Empire, was not content to let the river meander where it wanted; she was determined to shape and steer the river.

If you want publishers to *beg* to publish your book – you can have that – but first you must think like Maria Theresa and regulate your river.

Most authors don't think like this, though. They allow an unwieldy water flow to control their direction – sometimes the water levels are high, and sometimes they are low, sometimes the river is wide, sometimes it's narrow. The river meanders and the author follows. The river is in charge and it tells the author where to go.

"Oh! Maybe I'll write about health and wellness," the author thinks one day.

"People always tell me I should tell the story of my years in Djibouti – maybe I should write about that," she thinks the next.

"I've always wanted to run a retreat. Maybe I could do one in Belize."

The ideas come in at crooked angles and the author thinks: "I'll just follow the path of my true heart's desire. I trust the universe."

Well, yup, okay, I get it. I trust the universe too and I love listening to the whispers, but a little of Maria Theresa's strategic thinking would go a long way to get publishers begging to publish you, and that's what I want to share in this book.

On our cruise we visited Bratislava, Budapest, and Belgrade – three powerful capital cities along the Danube, all of which were strengthened by the regulation of the river. But that trickle down effect? It came straight from Vienna.

You don't know yet what your Bratislava, Budapest, and Belgrade will be – but if you can learn to straighten your river, make it deeper and more navigable, and learn to control its power, you will not only strengthen yourself, but you will be one with the flow of the water, positively affecting people, families, and cities in your path.

When you learn to regulate your river, you can change the world.

CHAPTER ONE

Why Publishers Aren't Begging to Publish You Now

Dani read *Jonathan Livingston Seagull* at twenty-five years old and she knew it was her life's mission to share a story that was just as compelling. She spent the next twenty-five years looking for her story. Dani was an ad executive and a small business owner. She travelled the world and while she never had kids, she brought her nieces and nephews the best gifts from her travels and earned the "cool aunt" title. She wore Doc Martin boots well into her forties and no one ever knew what color her hair would be next. Dani lived overseas in her twenties. Did a stint in the Peace Corps and another for a year at an ashram in the northern part of India near the Pakistani border.

Every year on her birthday, Dani reread *Jonathan Livingston Seagull*, the bestselling book by Richard Bach that had sent her on her journey. It was a fast read and she never tired of it.

Dani decided to spend her fortieth birthday alone, on a small boat, in Ha Long Bay in Vietnam. She was on a couples' cruise of all things (it was the only one available on the day she wanted to sail) and so she found herself single, surrounded by forty and fifty-something couples, in possibly the most beautiful location in the world. Ha Long Bay is actually listed as one of the New Seven Wonders of the World.

The boat was large enough for two dozen passengers and most of them seemed to sleep until the first smell of Pho around 9 a.m. But Dani got up at 5 a.m. on her fortieth birthday and found her way to the sundeck. It was already warm even though it was still dark. She unrolled the striped yellow towel onto the teakwood floor of the roof and laid down to meditate. The ship was ghost silent and after a year in the ashram, Dani could meditate for hours like a boss.

As soon as she closed her eyes, she felt the mountains of the bay wrap around her and each point on her chakra line light up. A flood of golden light poured through her crown chakra to the tips of her toes. She was floating in and out of consciousness and was filled with such a deep bliss she thought she might vomit from the intensity of the joy.

Dani felt her body split in two right down the middle and a high-speed film of an idea flooded her. It was *her* Jonathan Livingston Seagull! She asked, believed, and now on the deck of some weird boat in the middle of a strange bay in the heart of darkness, she received. Bam! The mountains were singing the story to her. It would be illustrated but for adults. It would be allegorical but practical. *The mountains* would be named as the author – she could see the cover and her name wasn't even there! It felt amazing to know every detail of her book. She wanted more downloads from the universe *and* she wanted to get up and write the whole book right now.

She was torn between staying in this dance with God and leaping into a new dance with man. This was the best birthday present *ever*! She broke out of the trance to write some notes and as she was writing, it was like someone was moving her hand. She had come off her striped towel and she was writing, but she was still in communion with spirit. It was like that all day and into the next. Before she got off the boat, she had most of the book written, a plan for related programs, and she even picked out a spot in Vietnam for her retreats. She created a vision board on an app on her phone despite the almost complete lack of Wi-Fi for everyone else on the ship.

This was her life's work and she knew it with total certainty! On her fortieth birthday, Dani had nothing but gratitude.

When I talked to Dani, it was a few weeks before her fiftieth birthday. She told me this story with a little sadness tingeing the gratitude now. It had almost been a decade, and the dream of her *Jonathan Livingston Seagull* story hadn't died, but it certainly wasn't a reality.

Dani's nieces and nephews were teenagers now, and they just thought she was a weird dreamer, like the inventor guy in *Back to the Future*. Her aqua hair was still fun but it didn't match the clothes that now fit her filled-out figure. She knew she had a song in her heart to sing but it was getting kind of embarrassing now. She didn't want everyone to see her as a flake.

People liked the story she wrote in Vietnam but it didn't catch on like Richard Bach's book. She had written and re-written it. Started a Facebook group for fans. She trained as a life coach. Attended Landmark Forum. She even got certified as a massage therapist and gave all of her massage clients a copy of the book. She had tried to do some retreats but no one signed up.

Dani was tired. In her dark moments, she felt like a fraud and a failure. But then there were these moments of optimism when she remembered the Ha Long Bay trip and what that download from the universe felt like. She knew she could be the next Elizabeth Gilbert or Richard Bach if only she could get a publisher to see her brilliance.

She wouldn't give up.

Not as long as there was a song in her heart.

Not as long as spirit spoke through her and pushed her forward.

Not as long as there was hope that she could be a channel for hope and healing.

And that's why Dani needed me. She needed me because she needed to know what it would take to get a publisher to beg to publish her book. Because Dani had *work* to do on this planet and Dani wasn't going to give up because it was hard.

I showed her what it would take to unlock the Hungarian puzzle box of making a difference with your message. I showed her what it would take to get any publisher to beg to publish her book. And I'm going to show that to you too in the following pages.

Before I show you how to get any publisher to beg to publish your book, I need to explain the simple and somewhat brutal reasons why publishers aren't banging down your door now (no matter how good your idea is, how good of a writer you are, or how many times spirit has whispered in your ear that you must get this message to the masses).

In my experience, there are six simple reasons publishers don't commit to unknown authors and take the dive into helping them make a difference with their message (even if it's obvious to everyone that you've got potential to be the next big thing that's ever happened to the personal development world and they could get in early on something huge if they would just take the risk and teach you what to do. Step aside Brené Brown and Elizabeth Gilbert!)

Note that the reasons publishers will tell you for not wanting to publish you (Your platform isn't big enough. We don't see people buying books on this topic right now. Something is missing and it needs a rewrite.) are generally just excuses to let you down easy.

I know because I have been on the other side of the rejection process and I have sat at the table (and ... err ... ummm bar) with acquisitions editors from the Big 5 and agents placing books at the Big 5 publishing houses and I can tell you, that isn't what we are talking about. Though if we get an author in front of us with a book that won't work, we will swear up and down that our hands are tied, the timing just isn't right for us, but we are sure their book will find a great home somewhere else.

All of that changed when I started The Author Incubator back in 2013. That's when I started to see the real reasons publishers don't commit to unknown authors:

Reason One: **The Hook Headache** – In your

mind you are thinking how good a writer you are will determine if a publisher wants your book, but the truth is, writing can be cleaned up by editors. The issue isn't whether you are a good enough writer or even if you have a good enough idea. The issue is whether you can *share* your idea with a sexy enough hook so that non-marketing-oriented publishing professionals will know what to do with your book so that copies get sold. The even bigger problem is that bad authors (undesirable authors) think it's their publisher's job to figure out the positioning for the book. That is *your* job as an author – your *main* job – even more important than writing the book! And a publisher can smell in seconds if you have a hot hook. If not, they can't waste time trying to do your job for you.

Reason Two: **The Snobbiness Situation** – Being the cool kid in the publishing world can't be underrated. Scoring the next Liz Gilbert book or Beyoncé's break out self-help title holds a lot of cachet in circles in the know. Random unknown author? Just doesn't have the cool factor and the publishing industry is nothing if not snobby. One of the top questions an agent or publisher is asking is: What will other people in the industry think? Will this raise or lower my status?

Reason Three: **The Pretty Problem** – Attractive authors sell more books. This is the truth. Like it or not. If you are unattractive, overweight, don't dress well, are not well-spoken, won't look good on TV if the publisher gets you media gigs, if you have a weird lisp or a lazy eye, you just aren't media-genic enough for a publisher to take a risk on. There is still a huge celebrity factor to this game. You don't have to be a supermodel, but you do need to hit a certain level of attractive-ness.

Reason Four: **The Neediness Nightmare** – Are you going to be an annoying author to work with? Publishers can smell that from a mile away. For instance, if you send in a propos-al when the instructions say you have to go through an agent. You can have the best idea on the planet and you aren't going to get picked up

– why? Because you are going to be needy! Needy is so not fun for publishers. If you *want* them to publish you, you are starting with a neediness factor of eight and it only goes up from there. You need a sub-five neediness factor to be even remotely attractive.

Reason Five: **The Platform Problem** – See if you can follow. Publishers make money from selling books. Employees of publishers get to keep their jobs when the books they work on make money. A small percentage (less than 6 percent) of your fans will buy your book. So the bigger your platform, the more accurately a publisher can estimate book sales. This reduces their risk which gives them the confidence to pitch their boss on why they need your book.

Reason Six: **The Bandwidth Block** – Publishers and agents only have so many hours in the day. Once they commit to an author, the time is gone. A really busy agent or imprint might only work with thirty or forty authors a year. Saying yes to you means saying no to someone else. It's a business based on placing bets strategically on which authors will succeed. Saying yes to you means the death of possibility of a bigger fish.

Yikes. Horrible list, huh? Remember though, most publishers aren't thinking about this stuff consciously – it's all sort of playing out in the background of their minds and in the landscape of the industry. Knowing this gives you a huge advantage to getting a top publisher to beg for your book.

Okay, now we have covered the big reasons why you don't have a big-name publisher already. Let's get to work on changing that.

In order for publishers to "wake up" to the amazing potential you have as a leader in the self-development movement and literally *beg* you to be on their list you have to do four things:

1. You have to shoot down or override the unconscious objections publishers have to seeing you as mainstream material.
2. You have to make publishers chase you and earn the right to be your publisher. You have to paint a picture for them of what it's

going to be like for them when you are their top-selling author.

3. You have to make them feel like you don't need them, and that they are going to *lose* the chance to be your publisher if they don't take action.

4. You have to make them feel like publishing you and investing the company's resources in making you a star is *their idea*.

Did you notice what's not on this list?

Whining, begging, bitching, complaining, or creating PowerPoint decks to convince them you will be the next big thing and they are missing out on an incredible opportunity.

Why?

Because when it comes to commitment from a publisher, convincing never works.

As you will learn in this book, the most important paradigm shift to make any publisher you want beg to publish your book is to fully understand this: "The prize never chases."

Listing all the reasons they should publish you will do nothing to create the attraction and need for you to be on their list of authors that we're going for here.

Okay so how do you flip the switch that makes them hunt you down and offer you a contract?

1. Stop *needing* them to publish you.
2. Take control of your own intellectual property.
3. Make them compete for you (and refuse to compete for them). If you're too easy to have, they are not going to want you.

And then, if everything we've talked about in this book doesn't light a fire under the publisher's ass to pick you, it's time to go nuclear. And that means you publish yourself and formally let this idea go.

When should you do this? Well that part is going to be up to you, but the path to a traditional publishing deal is simply never a fast one. So, if you are committed to getting a publisher to beg for your book, you are committing to at least a two-year horizon, maybe longer. Now, in those two years, you won't be sitting idly by, so the first step is to understand what it will take to get them to beg and offer you a deal that is worthy of *your* attention.

Once you understand what that is going to take and why, you might decide you are going to have to push the button and move on. We'll talk about what to do in that case as well.

And honestly, that's no big tragedy because you're going to discover that when you really understand how the publisher's mind works, it gets a lot easier to get the outcome you want from your book with or without the brand name publisher.

Confident, powerful authors have a lot more options in the elitist traditional publishing world than mousy, needy authors do. (And I promise, how good your ideas are and how good you are as a writer is only a tiny part of this!)

A lot of authors-in-transformation decide that understanding this world is too hard and that they will just hope someone spots them as the diamond in the rough they are. Don't be that person.

Maya Angelou said, "There is no greater agony than bearing an untold story inside you."

I believe her.

What I am about to teach you in this book is going to be hard and a lot of it is going to shock you, but it is a process I have guided hundreds of people through. Those people were not smarter than you. They didn't have better ideas than you. They weren't better writers than you.

What they may be, however, is more committed to helping their readers than you. Because if this is about serving your own ego, you will fail.

But if you are as passionate about your readers as Jill Angie is about helping runners of all shapes, sizes, and speeds to achieve their running dreams; or as passionate as Cassie Parks is about helping people identify and create their champagne life through the law of attraction; or as passionate as Sharon Pope is about helping people find the love they most deeply desire and deserve, then you can do this too.

Don't spend hours talking about what you are going to do in the future. Start doing it today. This is simpler and so much more effective than wishing things were different than they are. What you will learn in this book is that you can *go for it* – big! Right now! And, at the same time, set yourself up to have publishers begging to feature you in their advertising, to put posters of your book in bookstores, to sell the movie rights to your story, and so much more.

Remember Dani from the beginning of the chapter. She's fifty-two now and she still doesn't have a traditional publishing deal. I know that's not a great selling point considering the title of the book! But her book is finished and it is in book stores.

Dani shut down her massage therapy business about nineteen months ago now as I write this. She didn't have time to keep her massage busi-

ness going now that she is running those retreats in Vietnam that she planned over a decade
ago. Dani owns a retreat center in a little town
called Hoi An not too far from Ha Long Bay. She
goes there every other month with her clients
and spends the rest of the time at her house near
the beach in Encinitas.

Her nieces and nephews like to crash there when
she is in Vietnam.

Dani is officially the cool aunt again now that her
business took off. The message of Ha Long Bay is
a part of her movement to bring her clients back
to nature and to the source of their true essence.

Dani's clients are burnt-out corporate execu-
tives who enjoy her kinesthetic approach. What
Dani realized is that massage, reiki, and being in
nature – specifically in Asia for whatever reason
– were all a part of how she could solve her clients' problem which was really reconnection to
source. They didn't know that, of course. What
they tell Dani is they have been stuck in the same

job for over a decade, they are sick of it, and want to change careers.

Dani's clients find her through her books – she's got two out now – and when they come to Vietnam, they know they will leave with their career change plan. And they do. But what Dani knows is that they will also leave with a plan to reconnect with spirit and when they do this, they will find joy and peace in their current career or their new one.

Dani is making a difference with her message. And she is finally making a living that is as good as her ad executive days. She knows soon there will be a publisher begging to publish her next book, and she knows if the deal is good enough – she just might take it.

That is the exact position I want you to be in at the end of this journey we will go on together.

CHAPTER TWO

How to Get a Killer Literary Agent to Represent You

Let's talk about literary agents. If you want to get publishers begging to work with you, you are going to need an agent, so you should understand how they work and what motivates agents.

You are probably more familiar with real estate agents than literary agents, right? And if you remember, real estate agents generally only make money when a house is bought or sold. Residential real estate agents also tend to have the crappiest of schedules. For the most part, buyers want to look at houses at night and on weekends.

And for the most part, there is no guarantee the time they spend away from their family showing houses will result in a sale. Many buyers are not serious.

Good agents have a few things in common. First, the best agents will only work with sellers – and not just any seller, but a seller with a hot property.

If given the choice to show six properties to a single, unemployed, twenty-three-year-old, first time buyer or to list a desirably located three-bedroom bungalow owned by a couple in their thirties pregnant with their third child, the smart agent would represent the couple.

It just doesn't make sense to spend a ton of time on something where you aren't going to get paid. Agents know a good starter home, in a nice neighborhood, will almost certainly sell in the six-month window and will be worth investing their time, energy, and money on.

Our unmarried tire kicker *could* be sitting on a $50 million trust fund, it's true. But as an agent, you have to be smart about the time you use for your clients to maximize your revenue potential, especially since you are almost certainly going to be working primarily nights and weekends.

Your Agent Isn't Running a Charity for Wanna-Be Stars

It's the same for literary agents. Any literary agent worth her weight in salt can't spend time on projects that are unlikely to find a home. A literary agent only makes money when your book sells to a publisher. If the publisher pays you $100,000, the agent makes $15,000. If the book doesn't sell, the agent doesn't make money.

Your first job is to sell an agent on why they should represent you – why are you more like the couple in their thirties on baby number three than the probably flaky singleton?

Here's what would convince almost any agent it was worth their time to work with you – for free – on the hope that someday they will make money:

- You are famous – and by that, I mean you have 1,000,000 plus followers in social media or on your email list. You have a reality TV show or a major column in a national publication.
- You have a big idea that has traction – you are the Queen of a Specific Mountain – you have actual, real achievements.
- You have credentials so your agent won't be embarrassed by you when she pitches you to a traditional publisher.
- You are well-spoken and attractive.
- You "get" the marketing game, have a history of making investments that have paid off.
- Table stakes: you are at least a good writer, ideally a great one. If you aren't, you know it and are prepared to hire accordingly.
- You are 0 percent entitled, whiny, or victimy.
- You get what you are bringing to the table and you know if this agent isn't a fit, another one will be.
- You are 100 percent sure you are going to be successful with or without this agent.

Notice how small a role your idea plays in this list. You know how in real estate they say it's all about location, location, location. That tiny bungalow in a great neighborhood, with lots of jobs and schools nearby is better than a mansion in the middle of nowhere. Well, for the world of literary agents, "location" is your platform – the number of people you reach.

Be Like Bey

Think about Beyoncé. She gets whatever she wants because she literally owns her fans. She can release an album at midnight on a weekday with no press release and go Platinum in an hour. There is zero risk for her agent (and her publisher, but we'll get to that in a minute). Now I get we can't all be like Beyoncé, but you want to avoid the alternative – which is basically the literary equivalent of being a booty call.

Sometimes you can find an agent who is either super hard up for business or worse, you can just do a really good job of selling yourself to someone who is fully booked and you can get that agent (who is really a bad fit) to say yes to working with you. An agent will have you sign a contract "tying you up" for 6 months to a year. That means any publishing deal that comes through during that time window, the agent will get 15 percent of.

Most of the time, your agent will pitch your idea quickly. Think about it, if that thirty-year-old couple wanted their bungalow listed, a real estate agent wouldn't sit on it for six months, they would list it pretty much right away. Your agent has a few go-to publishers and partners they have done a bunch of deals with. They can't mention your book to those people until the contract is signed. When the contract is signed, they will want to get a deal done as quickly as possible because that is how they get paid! Remember, no one likes to work for free and psychologically it's hard to do a good job working for free – until revenue is inevitable like it would be with Beyoncé.

Now if your book doesn't get picked up pretty quickly, the agent, who only has so many hours in the day in which to generate her income, feed her family, and take care of herself, literally *has* to start blowing you and your project off. Even if she likes you. It just doesn't make sense to keep putting a ton of time in on something that isn't going to generate an income. She isn't running a charity, right?

And this is why most people hate their agents. Because now, you have an option – let your project die, or hustle to do a deal that your agent will take 15 percent of even though you don't feel like she deserves it.

Do you see how fucked up this situation is?

Recently, I was in a position to hire a financial advisor. I met with this guy who was well-dressed and super friendly. He came to my house. Had my husband and I fill out a bunch of forms and then suggested what products we should invest in.

What I loved about this guy was that we didn't have to pay him. He would basically do all this work for us for free and then whatever we invested in, he would take a small piece of that.

In my head, it was like – if we make money, he makes money! Cool!

The Fiduciary Standard

I signed off on some major investments pretty quickly and I was so excited I told my best friend Brooke.

"No, seriously, you have to talk to my client Mary!"

She told me in no uncertain terms I was not to sign another piece of paper without talking to Mary Sterk, a financial advisor from South Dakota.

Mary is an artist with a giggle. She's blonde and smiley and has a mid-west politeness to her that just doesn't scream "financial genius" from across the room so much as it does "cute blonde."

But that's from across the room. As soon as she opened her mouth I knew she was a force to be reckoned with.

Mary explained to me that she charged her clients – a *lot* – to work with her. I wasn't loving that idea and I was happy with my guy. He wore bow ties for god's sake! But then Mary explained to me, "There are two standards – the 'suitability' standard and the 'fiduciary' standard. Your guy is set up to meet the suitability standard."

"In a nutshell," Mary continued, "the suitability standard means the advisor has to know the client well enough to make a suitable recommendation. The problem with this is that if there are three products that are all suitable for the client, the advisor has no regulations against picking the one that pays the most commission."

"Oh," I said as a knot formed in my stomach. "What's the other thing called?"

"The fiduciary standard is what I work under," she explained. "This means that I don't just tell my clients what would be 'suitable' for them, I am required to always do what is in the best interest of my client. I have to follow a documented process to prove that I selected something that wasn't just suitable or appropriate but literally in the best interest of the client. Generally, the compensation is level regardless of what they recommend so there is no financial incentive for an advisor to recommend one product over another."

Not long after this conversation a few things happened:

1. I fired the guy with the bow tie.
2. I hired Mary and started happily paying her – a lot! – to help me make financial decisions in my *best interest* – not just something suitable that makes the agent the most money.
3. I convinced Mary to write a book with us. You should go get it – it's called *Ready to Pull the Retirement Trigger?* So good! (Yup, Brooke was right!)

What I realized almost immediately when Mary started explaining her industry is that literary agents for the past 300 years or so have been working in this suitability model. They aren't screwing over their clients – I think bow-tie guy was making perfectly reasonable suggestions for me. But they are making suggestions that will generate an income for them – because honestly, nothing else would make sense. What, was he supposed to work for free? Just like bow-tie guy was incentivized to pick the products that he thinks will be a terrific fit for me that also make him the most money, most agents are incentivized to pitch your book to the people they know and then sit on it if it doesn't sell on the odd chance it sells later or through some other process.

But do you really want your career and your movement in the hands of someone who will act "suitably"? Wouldn't you rather have a Mary Sterk in your corner acting in your absolute highest and best interest? Someone who was being fairly compensated *no matter what* to look out for you so she had a reason to really crunch the numbers and look at the options?

This, by the way, in celebrity circles is called a manager. I think most people get an agent and *think* they have a manager because they don't understand these two different standards.

I think you need a manager before you get an agent because I suspect you don't know what you are doing. You have a goal and you don't know how to get there. You see that other people have gotten there, but you don't know the path for yourself and you are hoping a publisher or an agent is going to help you carve that path. That isn't their job.

Based on countless, exhausting conversations with literary agents, I'd hazard a guess that most agents don't even get this point. Like real estate agents who sign up to work long hours, mostly nights and weekends, with no guaranteed pay, most literary agents themselves don't have a great plan for generating revenue. They are often broke and incredibly non-strategic about how they grow their own business.

Think about the smartest business people you know. How many of them have set up their business to be like a lottery where their success depends almost entirely on someone else's brilliance and where they do most of their work on spec only getting paid a fraction of the time?

The truth is, the world needs a *lot* more managers and coaches to help artists and healers bring their messages to the masses and it needs a lot fewer agents to capitalize on the hard work of the talent. The model is flipped because people have a weird relationship with money.

It's like me and the bow-tie guy. I was ready to invest millions of dollars with him because it was "free." If I hadn't met Mary, I wouldn't have realized that sure, I didn't have to pay up-front for his time, but that decision of wanting his "suitable" advice for free could have cost me millions and taken me years, maybe decades longer, to be ready to pull the retirement trigger.

So be careful what you wish for. You might get an agent, but they might not be working for you in the way you think.

Here's what I want you to remember from this chapter.

1. You almost certainly need an agent to get a great publishing deal.
2. You only want to get an agent when you know it's a slam dunk for them to make lots of money.

Until you can be a slam dunk for an agent, you need to focus on becoming a slam dunk. If you need help with that, you get a manager and/or a coach.

Once you understand what's your job, what's an agent's job, and when you need to bring an agent on your team, you can set yourself up to have publishers begging to publish your book and that's what I want to finally talk about in our next chapter.

CHAPTER THREE

Getting a Sacred Yes from a Traditional Publisher

My grandmother died in 1987, but every year, she still gets my sisters and me a scratch-off lottery ticket. My mom is in charge of the shopping on her behalf. Every year, when our kids have opened all the presents, the wrapping paper has been stuffed into garbage bags, and the boxes collapsed into themselves, my older sister will make coffee and my mom will dig out some coins and the scratch-off cards from Nonni.

We're usually exhausted by that point so we huddle around a small table in a back room, hiding from the noise and the children. There is a tickle of anticipation and excitement as we begin scratching away.

My mom is no slouch when it comes to picking scratch-off cards. These aren't the $1 cards with the max prize of $1,000. No. My mom goes for the Lucky 777s Tripler. It's a $10 card with a prize pool of $177,777. Big money in scratch-off land.

It always seems like one of the three of us should win *something*. And sometimes one of us will win $10. In thirty Christmases of scratch-offs since my grandmother died, we've never gotten my mom her money back on those scratch-off cards.

And it makes sense when you look at the odds. We get three lottery tickets. The odds of winning $10 are 1 in 3.57 which means sometimes we get $10 of my mom's money back and rarely much more. The odds of winning the $177,777? One in 392,154!

Still, there is a certain excitement to the potentiality of winning. We keep playing even though losing is virtually guaranteed.

It's a Crapshoot

For us, it's been thirty years. For the publishing industry, they have been playing high-stakes scratch-off games every day since 1640.

"It's the way this business has run since 1640," says Al Greco, a professor of marketing at Fordham University. That is when 1,700 copies of the Bay Psalm Book were published in the colonies. "It was a gamble, and they guessed right because it sold out of the print run. And ever since then, it has been a crap shoot."

I think it's hard to really understand an industry built around a crap shoot. But that is the nature of the publishing business.

Not too long ago one of our authors, Sophie Sabbage, wrote a book called *The Cancer Whisperer*. She published the eBook with us and pursued a pretty aggressive PR campaign for her launch as many of our authors do.

Sophie had a blog at the time, with a couple thousand subscribers, but not much else.

She was no Beyoncé! She is a beautiful writer with an important message (you should go get her book right now), but from a gambling perspective, the chance of Sophie's book selling millions of copies was about as good as me winning the Lucky 777 Tripler.

Recently I had the chance to sit down with Sophie's agent and a representative from her publisher for almost two hours. I asked each of them – with no list, no marketing strategy, no proven investment track with a positive ROI – why did you take Sophie's book? Her eBook, which we had published, sold a fraction of what other titles had sold. What was it that made you think this was a good investment of your time and for your company?

Remember, her agent wouldn't make a cent unless she could sell the manuscript to a publisher.

And the publisher wouldn't make a cent unless her team could sell the book to bookstores.

Ultimately, they both needed Sophie to have the marketing muscle to get books *out* of the bookstores – selling to consumers is *always* the author's job – even though the publisher keeps 90 percent of the profits for themselves.

The answers were illuminating.

"I loved it," they said.

"It was so beautifully written."

"It touched my heart even though I didn't have cancer."

They gushed over Sophie's writing. But I was on the other side of the video conference call scratching my head. Sophie is a beautiful writer, it's true, but there must have been something more scientific behind their decision. Surely, there are thousands, maybe millions of writers that are just as good as Sophie.

Why THIS Book?

Sophie is great on the media, so I asked to talk to her publicist. "Were you a part of the decision to take Sophie's book? Was it because you knew you could get her a ton of press and she'd blow up the airwaves?"

"Nope. I wasn't brought on board until after the decision was made," said the publicist.

This was an enigma wrapped in a mystery.

Were they just holding industry secrets close, I wondered.

There was some secret sauce and they just didn't want to tell little ol' me?

I was sure that must be it, so I reached out to a stalwart of the publishing industry. A man I'll call Eric, in his seventies with fifty years of experience with mainstream publishers right in the heart of Manhattan. As a distributor, he had perspective into every single publishing house.

I told him the story and begged him to help me understand.

"Did you see Sophie's publishing house also got the Obama deal last month?" he asked me by means of explanation.

I admitted I hadn't been following.

"Bidding started at $20 million," he said "But the rumor at the London Book Fair was that his advance ended up at $62 Million."

I quickly ran the numbers in my head.

An advance is the *author's money* paid to them upfront. This is what the publisher believes the book will generate in the first year. An author generally makes $1 a book. So, a $62 million-dollar advance would be 62,000,000 books sold in year one.

"Hmmm," I thought. "I know that's more votes than he got! I know it's world-wide rights and all but is that even possible? There are only 15 books that have done that in all of history!"

Eric mentioned Obama's other books had sold more than 4 million copies.

"Will they make money if he sells 4 million copies again? I'm running the numbers and I don't see it. What am I not getting?"

Eric laughed the laugh of experience. "They are snobs," he said. "They'll lose money on this deal, but they get the bragging rights, and that's what they paid for."

I shook my head in disbelief. This is how the world works, I thought.

They will take a *guaranteed* money-loser from Obama and a virtually guaranteed money-loser from Sophie because they liked the books? They want bragging rights? These are business cases?

The End of Big Publishing

No wonder Seth Godin has declared the publishing industry dead. "Ideas aren't going away soon, and neither are words. But, as the ecosystem dies, not only will the prevailing corporate systems around the paper book wither, but many of the treasured elements of its consumption will disappear as well ... and many in traditional book publishing will find their particular skills no longer valued the way they used to be."

There isn't a lot of logic we can apply here, but what I've pieced together is this:

Sophie got some great media coverage for her book launch. Her agent is a delightful, talented, heart-centered soul who was just touched and captivated by Sophie's words and her work. Who knows, maybe they had a soul-contract to work together in this lifetime. Honestly, it wouldn't surprise me.

Her agent took a risk. The same way, if she was a real estate agent, she might have taken a risk on that single twenty-three-year-old who was thinking of buying a house. She "took a flyer" on Sophie, knowing she might put work in and not get paid.

She pitched Sophie's book to an editor friend in the industry whom she had done other deals with and that editor saw the potential. It wasn't an amazing business decision; it was an emotional one made through luck and friendships and not a ton of business savvy from what I can tell.

Since most books lose money for publishers, Sophie's probably will too – I don't have inside information there and I hope I'm wrong – but we know between 1:7 and 1:10 books generate a profit for the publisher, and so they took a risk on her because they liked her.

I am thrilled for Sophie. I want her book on every bookshelf in every home in every country around the world. But my honest assessment is – she won the Lucky 777s Tripler. She is the 1 in 392,154.

You can focus on your craft, be a brilliant writer, practice resilience, network like a queen, and not get this result. In fact, you most likely won't. You will most likely win $10 for every 1 in 3.57 scratch-off tickets you buy.

Pointing to data from the book-tracking firm R.R. Bowker on the more than three million new titles published last year, Professor Greco reminds us, "If you publish a book today, you're going to be one of 8,473 for the day. What sort of attention can you possibly get in the marketplace even if this company does a spectacular job?"

All Magic Comes with a Price

I know I'm not convincing you. You are like me at the end of an exhausting Christmas day, chomping at the bit to get my hands on that scratch-off ticket. You stare the odds in the face and say "Bring it universe! I am ready to win."

I understand the feeling. And I'm still going to try to talk you out of it before I tell you how you can get it. Because you *can* get a traditional publishing deal – I can tell you exactly how to do it – and I will – and it is guaranteed to work – but before I tell you, you have to understand the cost of what you are asking for.

My eleven-year-old son and I watch this TV show called "Once Upon a Time," where Rumpelstiltskin, one of the main characters, says, "All magic comes with a price, dearie." I want you to understand the deal you would be signing up for.

By now, you know the financial breakdown.

A traditional publisher is going to take the lion's share of revenue generated from your intellectual property and marketing. You think the thoughts, you write the book, you market to consumers through speaking, blogging, being a podcast guest and media source.

Here's the question I want you to ask yourself very seriously:

What would make it worth giving up 50 – 90 percent of your revenue to a publisher?

I can think of four main categories and I'm going to discuss each and share

Myth One: A Publisher Will Pay for Me to Publish. And as Every "Real" Author Knows, "You Don't Pay to Publish."

This whole idea that it's free to publish with a traditional publisher cracks me up. It is *sooooo* much more expensive. Look, it's true that with a publisher there are no upfront financial costs, and there's usually some kind of advance against royalties.

But the advance doesn't mean they are paying you, it's your own damn money they are just giving you in advance of you earning it. It's like getting a paycheck for the whole year on January 1 and then having to go to work every day with no new money coming in. Do you know how demotivating that is?

Every new book represents a risk to the publisher, who is gambling tens of thousands of dollars that it will sell enough copies to earn a profit. Most books barely cover their costs or at best earn a small profit, and this is particularly the case with books by unknown authors. Therefore, publishers try to keep costs down by offering small advances. And even though small, advances almost always lose money.

So you are agreeing to an extra low wage in exchange for getting all your pay up front at the beginning of the year. And why would they be willing to make this deal?

Because they will keep the other 90 percent of your salary for themselves!

You are, in fact, paying much, much more to publish if your book is successful. The only way in this scenario you are not paying to publish is if your book doesn't sell.

In other words – when you say, "I don't pay to publish," you are betting on your book to be a massive failure – but at least it's a failure you didn't back with your own money.

Most of our print books sell in paperback so I'm going to give you a basic calculation of what it would take for you to "not pay to publish" with a traditional publisher.

Let's take a $14.95 trade paperback where the author as standard receives 7.5 percent retail. That translates to:

$7.48 to the bookseller

$5.83 to the publisher

$0.95 to the author

$0.17 to the agent

Let's say you got a standard "good" advance of $10,000.

Let's say in a year you sell the predicated 10,526 copies in order for you to "earn out your advance."

You will have $0 new dollars – because you already got paid for all that work before you did it, remember? *Yay*!

And your publisher will have $61,366.58 in shiny new pennies.

Alternatively, let's say you invested half of the money you and your publisher made in a year – that's a total of your $10K plus your publisher's $61K divided by two – around $35,000 in your budget.

Let's say you and I sat down and came up with a plan for you to spend $35,000 wisely on publishing and marketing your book, right? And you sold those same 10,526 copies on your own. Then you would have $6.95 in gross revenue from your book to keep yourself or a total of

$73,155.70. After your expenses of $35,000, that's $38,155.70 for you to keep. Almost 4 times what you got from the publisher and oh my god how much more satisfying.

Now of course if your book only sells 200 copies, then a traditional deal would be great.

You get $10,000 when you really only earned $190. You are up almost $9,800 on the house assuming they aren't asking for the money back which some publishers do these days.

The publisher gets $1,166 so they lose about $9K plus all their expenses for the services they provided - probably a $20K - $25K loss for the publisher all together.

Oh and your agent, let's not forget her, she put in about 100 hours on working with you. She's made $1500 back on the advance but now she has burned a bridge with this publisher and she's not super excited about your next book.

So saying you don't pay to publish is either a complete myth or a complete scam.

Either way, my vote is always for betting on yourself to win.

If this math is confusing, head over to www. YouDontPayToPublish.com for a free class with me where I'll explain this all slower and with visual aids!

For purposes of this book, we are going to bust the myth that you don't pay to publish when you do a traditional deal – in fact, you potentially pay a lot! Let's agree that saving on upfront costs to produce and market your book is not a good reason to go with a traditional publisher.

Myth Two: A Publisher Will Get Me More Sales

A lot of people think their publisher is going to do their marketing. Let's clear that up right away. Unless you are Dan Brown or J.K. Rowling, they won't be investing in advertising to consumers for your book – or even good placement in stores. Reaching the consumers to sell books is all on you.

Publishers do B2B marketing. Meaning they will sell your books INTO bookstores. It's your job to find consumers to buy them and get them out of bookstores, or else the bookstore orders get returned or remaindered. Both of which include you not making any money.

What publishers can do that you can't is get your books into stores. (I mean you can do this, but the cost in time and money is going to be way too high and not worth attempting.)

The problem with this advantage is that bookstores do appear to be dying – especially among non-fiction buyers who are searching for solutions to problems often when bookstores aren't even open.

As Seth Godin explains, "The bookstore as we know it is doomed, because many of these establishments are going to go from making a little bit of money every day to losing a little bit. The death of the bookstore is being caused by the migration to eBooks (it won't take all books to become 'e', just enough to tip the scale) as well as the superior alternative of purchase and selection of books online."

In fact, according to researchers at Foner Books, sales of print books on Amazon are outpacing bookstore sales 3:1.

Now your publisher will feature you in their sales catalog and on a website and they will pitch your book to book clubs and libraries. They might even do a press release that no one sees, but the truth is, this is not what's really going to move the needle – you are.

So again, for purposes of this book, we are going to bust this myth and assume you aren't going with a traditional publisher because of their help with sales.

Myth Three: A Publisher Will Provide Me an Established Professional Team

There are some talented people who work at publishing companies. Editors, designers, and publicists who believe in books. One of the best things about being published is having the opportunity to craft and polish your work with the aid of an experienced, sensitive professional.

But you need to ask yourself, who are these people working for? Remember, the trick is to follow the money. The publisher is fronting the costs for your book. Here are some of the services you get with a traditional publisher that you will have to pay for if you do it on your own (or learn how to do yourself):

- book design (including cover design, layout and typography)
- editing (several stages)
- typesetting and proofreading (several stages)
- cover brief and preparation of cover art (several stages)
- project management services to keep key people up to date
- cover copy, marketing copy, press release copy
- marketing plan
- proof and printing

I would estimate your publisher will spend at least $10,000 on you – maybe as little as $5,000 and as much as $20,000 depending on their overhead and company values. And that doesn't include the fact that they had to front you an advance.

They are spending this because *you* are their product. This work is their product development. And their employees ... well, that is the publisher's way of protecting their brand. They have made an investment in you, now they have to protect that investment.

The editors, designers, publicists, and marketing team aren't looking out for *you* – they aren't working for *you* – it's not *your* team! These people are protecting the interests of the people paying their salary – the publishing company.

Now, they are nice people, they are competent people (for the most part), and they aren't malicious people. They aren't going to screw you over. But they are going to put the needs and interests of their boss first. It's the only logical option.

So if there is a cover design or a title that might help you get more clients in your coaching practice (which does not impact the revenue of the publishing company) and a cover design or a title that might help sell more books (which does impact the revenue of the publishing company), guess which your editor or designer will recommend.

In fact, you won't even see the other options.

In fact, your "team" from the publishing company won't even ask about your business or revenue processes.

In fact, you and your publisher are working against each other without even knowing it.

A win-win occurs when two parties want the same thing. But you and your publisher want different things. They want lots of book sales at any cost to your brand and your bottom line. They want you to spend money and go on book signing tours even if no one comes to buy your books. They want you to spend hundreds of dollars to sell a single book because you spend and they profit.

Your publisher will push you to do more marketing and they will blame you when bookstores return your initial order after ninety days because it didn't sell. They will load you down with meaningless marketing tasks so they can tell their boss and other teams just how hard they are working to protect the company's investment in you and then, when your book doesn't sell (because remember, most don't), they will throw you under the bus. Oh, and if you happen to get dealt a Lucky 777 Tripler? They will for sure take the credit for the success.

The publishing team will tell you that it's hard to know what's going to work and what isn't, and the secret of successful promotion is to do a lot of different things in the hope that some of them will be effective. Oh and by the way, you are in charge of all that, so if it means you spend less time selling and serving clients, well, oh, well, you should have thought of that before you took the advance.

So there is myth three. Well and truly busted. *You* don't get a team when you work with a publisher. The publisher's team gets you. You are just a pawn in the game. If you really want to protect and exploit your own rights you need a team that is 100 percent aligned behind you. Who is compensated to protect your goals – not their own.

The Only Real Reason to Go with a Traditional Publisher Anymore

At the end of the day there is only one reason to go with a traditional publisher these days.

The one myth I can't bust.

The one reason it still makes sense to do a traditional publishing deal.

The one thing you need to be honest with yourself about.

THE SNOB FACTOR

The truth is, unless you publish with a traditional publisher, despite all the incredible costs and downsides, there are some outcomes you can't get on your own.

None of them have to do with making money or making a difference. All of them have to do with having a seat at the big kids' table and the value of that to you personally.

- A lot of national media outlets will ignore you without a traditional publisher.
- You are highly unlikely to be able to sell TV, movie, or magazine rights without a traditional publisher.
- You will not be eligible for many/most literary prizes including the *New York Times* Bestseller list. (See Chapter Five for more on that).
- If you are trying to get your own TV show – a traditional deal will help.
- Should you be applying for an extraordinary person visa with the US government, a traditional deal is the way to go.

These are the types of things a traditional deal can get you.

Still want it?

The Prize Never Chases

At the end of the day, if you still want a traditional publishing deal, then you need to know how to get them begging to work with you. You need the Obama deal where publishers are in a bidding war and they want you badly enough that they will pay *more* for your book than it can even be worth. And there is a way to make that happen.

Here is the answer you have been waiting for. Ready? I don't want you to miss it.

THE PRIZE NEVER CHASES.

This is how you get a traditional publishing deal. You stop wanting one. You stop needing one. You stop expecting a broken industry to save you like some messed-up fairy-tale Prince Charming.

Wait – but how do you not chase when this is what you want? You make yourself irresistible to them.

What do publishers care about?

Two things:

Prestige and selling books.

If you can't give them the Beyoncé or Obama names – and I'm guessing as fabulous as you are, if you are reading this book, you don't have that kind of cachet – then you need to give them book sales.

You (yes, you) need to go sell at least 10,000 copies of your book but ideally 35,000 copies. You need to get orders for these books in bulk. You need to collect credit card numbers and addresses and be ready to deliver these names to an agent or even publisher directly.

You are going to be completely prepared to keep 100 percent of your royalties. And then, if you want to give up 50-90 percent of those royalties to a publisher for some reason, you will have all the leverage you need to do that.

Put yourself in a position where you actually do have the power and you know how to use it! For more on how to do this see Chapter Eight on growth hacking. For now, just know it's absolutely possible.

If It Isn't a Win-Win, It's a No

A few months ago, I was flying to Lake Tahoe and I sat next to Howard Fineman. Howard is the global editorial director for *The Huffington Post* and appears regularly on NBC and MSNBC as a political commentator. For years, he was the chief political correspondent at *Newsweek*.

If anyone has an impressive media rolodex, it's Mr. Fineman!

Back in 2009, Fineman wrote a book published by Random House called *The Thirteen American Arguments: Enduring Debates That Define and Inspire Our Country.*

On the flight, he explained to me how the team at Random House put together a series of book signings to get the word out about the book. The bookstore signings didn't generate meaningful revenue. They couldn't! Run the numbers! A hugely successful book signing has probably twenty book sales. Maybe fifty if you are super lucky. Even if the publisher is making $10 a book, the cost to set up the signing is more than $500. And at $1 or $2 a book for the author, it is certainly not worth the author's time.

The book did sell though, after Fineman's appearances on John Stewart and Stephen Colbert's nightly shows. And how did those appearances come through? Well Fineman's rolodex of course! Now had he self-published, would his friends from those TV shows still welcomed him on? My guess is that they would have. But even if not, remind me why he called in the favor? Was it to make his publisher some money? Because it seems to me he did all the heavy lifting and the publisher did most of the profiting.

I think this is why I get so mad at the "You-don't-pay-to-publish" crowd I mentioned in Chapter Four. Because look, Fineman saved himself the upfront costs of publishing, but he did *pay* to publish. He gave up probably 90% of his revenue for what to me, does not seem to be 90 percent worth of value.

I'd rather see authors paying up front, owning their own intellectual property, and working with business managers (whom they pay) to make sure they fully exploit their own rights, instead of having publishers hold all the power.

I told Mr. Fineman that on the flight; he said he'd call when he was ready to write his next book.

CHAPTER FOUR

Never Pay to Publish!

Back in the 1990s, I worked on a book called *Aboard Air Force One*, by former Clinton White House staffer, Ken Chitester. Ken had a full-time job post-presidency as a publicist and professional communications guy. He wasn't going to quit his job and make a living as a writer with this book, but he did love to write and his stories from his days flying around with Bill Clinton were pretty damn entertaining.

Ken wrote some query letters to agents, put a proposal together, but the project wasn't going anywhere. Ken hired me as his editor and we polished up the manuscript quite a bit, but still, no bites.

A year went by and Ken called from Little Rock with news. "I've found a publisher!" he told me as his golden retriever, Camelot, barked at a squirrel in the background.

"Who is it?" I asked.

"They are called Fithian Press. It's a vanity house but...."

His voice trailed off.

Or maybe it didn't trail off ... but what I know for sure is that I didn't hear *anything* after the words "vanity house."

My heart sunk. "vanity house!" I fumed in my head! "Meaning the assholes who take out ads at the back of Rolling Stone magazine to sucker dumb people into giving them money? That's who you are publishing with?"

I didn't say it. But I knew it. He had given up and been sucked into a losing scheme. He had been suckered. And my editing work – all those hours of perfecting the book – they would be locked inside boxes in a garage in Little Rock, Arkansas for ten years until he cleaned out his garage and threw them out.

I was shattered.

Ken was my first author to go to a vanity press. I was used to Macmillan or Random House or Wiley or Penguin taking my books. Fithian Press felt like a smack in the face. I'd bury it on my resume lest anyone find out I worked on books that went through vanity press "publication" – if you can even call it that.

Back then, I was the Queen of the "You-Never-Pay-to-Publish" movement.

It was "Big 6 or Bust" as far as I was concerned (Big 5 now that Penguin and Random House got married).

I was right about Ken's book. It didn't sell. It didn't make a difference. And it was a *damn* good book!

In my head, the only way to make a difference was with a traditional book deal.

But that was back when I thought the purpose of writing and publishing books was to sell books. Ha! I know! That seems like it should be the goal, but let's talk about who wins with that kind of thinking.

With a traditional deal, most publishers will pay authors an advance of the author's own money. The publisher will say "Hey Ken! We think we can sell 10,000 copies of your book and we are willing to pay you $1 a book so we'll just give you that $10K now in exchange for the opportunity to exploit your intellectual property."

Ken is supposed to feel blessed for the opportunity and not pay attention to the fact that any publisher who believes *you* will make $10,000 enough to pay it to you in advance also believes they will make $90,000 from your book. (A 9:1 split is pretty standard. 8:1 is amazing and 1:1 is the best you can hope for and never with one of the Big 5.)

Have you ever heard the term "The house never loses"? It usually references Las Vegas casinos

– but the same is true in publishing. They might not win with every book but 9:1 odds mean, overall, publishers will make money and most authors will lose.

93 percent of traditionally published books make less than $1,000. And still! The house usually wins at the end of the day. What does that tell you about the other 7 percent? Chances of an author winning with a traditional deal are very low – about 7 percent – chances of the house winning are almost guaranteed. Boo!

As self-publishing has become easier and easier, the term Vanity Press has faded into a new term: Author-funded publishing. The shame and stigma of paying to publish has dissipated, and yet there are still those that wave the "You-never-pay-to-publish" flag I once so proudly carried.

As author-funded publishing has evolved through the democratization of publishing, so has another trend – the indies. Seth Godin and Gay Kawasaki have led the charge of the indies. Rather than pay to publish – these authors would do it themselves – they would *become* publishers.

Rather than pay companies like Fithian Press to publish their books, the indies would learn the mechanics of design, managing an editorial team, search engine optimization, Amazon search algorithms, pricing analysis, rights and translations work, and marketing strategy in addition to continuing to hone their skills as a writer.

"If guys like Fithian Press can figure it out," thought these bold "indies," "so can I!"

And the self-publishing revolution began in earnest. "Screw the vanity presses even with their fancy new names," was their rallying cry. The titans of author-funded publishing, Author Solutions, became enemy number one of the publishing world.

About a year ago, audiobook and business scalability expert James Tonn invited me into a community of these indie types I'd been reading about from my ivory tower. These were fiction authors called "Smarter Artists," a group run by self-publishing geniuses and all-around smart dudes, Johnny B. Truant and Sean Platt. Smarter Artist are mostly science fiction and romance novelists who raise high the "You-never-pay-to-publish" rallying cry.

I played "fly on the wall" for over twelve months before I formulated an opinion on the indie ethos, because the truth is, while we never charge people to publish at The Author Incubator, I do have several business partners and colleagues who *do* charge to publish and I have sent several of our #incubatedauthors to those colleagues.

The thinking from the Smarter Artist camp is that as a full-time author, it's your job to either figure out how to write a compelling book proposal and get a traditional publisher *or* to learn how to self-publish. (Often "Smarter Artists" do both.)

I understood the cry because it was one I'd felt a couple decades before when Ken told me he was paying a vanity publisher, but my perspective had changed in the years that passed.

While the "Smarter Artists" I was meeting were consumed with the goal of making a full-time six-figure income as a writer, the authors I had come to focus on working with had the goal of generating their income through coaching, consulting, and speaking.

I work with life coaches and other experts who often (though not always) enjoy writing, but not as much as they enjoy making a difference and changing people's lives. My authors exist to solve painful problems that keep people from living a life they love and writing is one way for them to connect with the people they are on the planet to serve.

They often write two or three books – one of our authors, Cassie Parks, even wrote seven books in about two years (between December 2014 and January 2017). But their main goal isn't to make a living as an author – it is to make a living from making a difference.

Books are amazing tools – but no matter how slowly you read, when you finish reading a book on weight loss, you haven't lost 100 lbs. When you finish reading a book about money mindset, you haven't attracted $10,000. When you finish reading a book on how to write a book, your book is not written.

I believe, and my authors believe: Truly making a difference means working directly and intensely with the readers who most connected with your message until they get the ultimate result or dream come true with the help of the author.

As a side note, you should know we never charge people to publish at The Author Incubator and when you do see us publish books, not only did we do that for free for our year long clients as a bonus, but we also give them 100 percent of their royalties. Years ago, I used to do a 50/50 revenue split on royalties and there are a handful of books with that deal – but what I came to realize is there is a conflict of interest when you split royalties, so I always give authors all of their money. If we collect a penny on their behalf it goes straight to the author – more on that in Chapter Four.

For now I want to talk about the idea "You Never Pay to Publish!"

When it comes to "real writers" – people who want to make a full-time income from the sale of books – there is no doubt in my mind "You don't pay to publish."

Why?

Well because these days, the job of being a full-time writer includes about 20 percent of your time writing and 80 percent of your time publishing. Alternatively, you can spend 80 percent of your time writing and give up 90 percent of your revenue to a traditional publisher. In other words ... if you decide *not* to learn how to become a publisher yourself, then you are agreeing to paying 80-90 percent of anything your ideas earn to someone else.

Now this presumes you *could* get a publishing deal – and look – you *could*. It can be a lot of work and take a long time, but if you want a publishing deal more than you want to learn how to be a great publisher yourself, you *can* do it. Other people – who are less good writers than you, who have less good ideas than you, who are less smart than you – have done it. And you can, too.

But the question is: which would you rather do? Work your ass off to get a publishing deal where you give most of your money to someone else? Or work your ass off to get great at publishing and have full control and keep all the money you earn?

Because those are the main options if we are going to agree that Real Writers Don't Pay to Publish.

And I'm in. After a year of careful listening, I am willing to concede this point – but I also have to say the cost of either choice is high, so choose wisely.

If you want to make money primarily from the sale of books in $1 or $10 increments, then take the time to make the right choice here.

And I really recommend becoming a part of the Smarter Artist community.

By the way, as I hinted earlier, lots of folks in that particular community advocate for a blend of learning how to self-publish and then leveraging your self-publishing success to get traditional deals and going back and forth between the two options. This is clearly the place of most freedom and leverage for people who make a full-time income from the sale of books.

However, this is not the situation the authors I work with most find themselves in.

Most of the authors I work with have spent years, often decades, learning a skill other than writing. Maybe it's how to grow and manage large teams, or how to bio-hack hormones to achieve optimal health, or how to practice mindfulness to create magical relationships.

Not only are they not focused primarily on the craft of writing like the Smarter Artist crew, they don't *want* to be. The craft of writing – of *being* a writer is a beautiful thing – but so is being a functional medicine doctor, or a relationship coach, or a business alignment expert. Few people have a zone of genius that includes both.

There is a very real toll on human lives if these powerful experts who are so good at what they do were to instead focus on something they aren't good at. Let's say one of my authors chose to learn the skills of self-publishing that the Smarter Artists so often advocate investing in. If they were to make even a ninety-day investment in building up these skills, most of my authors would be putting at least $50,000 in revenue from at least twenty clients at risk. The clients in turn would not get the help they needed and this could mean they end up divorced, or unemployed, or without that baby for months or maybe years.

My author would, after ninety days, have basic competency in a new skill that is probably not in their zone of genius. And their ideal reader will be further from hope, healing, and transformation.

I can't, in good conscience, advocate for that.

My mission on the planet is to help others bring their books into reality so that they might serve as beacons to attract the people these authors are most aligned to heal permanently.

My mission is most definitely not to encourage people to get good at doing something they weren't born to do!

So let me say this again – at The Author Incubator, we don't charge people to publish. Ever. There is no line-item in my revenue forecast that says "revenue from publishing" or "revenue from royalties" (well, except the royalties from the books I write). But I do recommend our authors pay to publish sometimes and I'm not ashamed of that.

Here are cases where I think it's a *huge* mistake to pay to publish:

- If you want to make a living as a full-time writer focused on the craft of writing and having full autonomy and creative rights over your intellectual property and you don't want to sell anything other than your books. (These are the true "Smarter Artists.")

- If you're retired or unemployed and/or have very little money. You don't want to be a full-time writer. And you don't have a book or platform that would sell to a traditional publisher. And you don't want to sell coaching, consulting – then you can write a book that is pure catharsis and publish it yourself without spending money like Ken had to back in the day.

- If you have a huge platform to exploit (500,000 fans or more) and it's not a good use of your time or energy to learn how to publish because of the opportunity cost. Sometimes it makes sense to give up 90 percent of your royalties to traditional publishers because your audience is so hungry for content. (This applies most often to our authors who are YouTube and reality TV show stars.)

But here are cases where I think it's a *huge* mistake *not* to pay to publish:

- If you are a life coach or other expert whose zone of genius is not writing and publishing, but is instead helping people and you want to use a professional-looking book to attract clients.
- You have a full-time job or a large savings. You don't want to be a full-time writer. But you don't have a book or platform that would sell to a traditional publisher.
- You are a sales and marketing-oriented person with a big following. You know you could get a fat advance from a traditional publisher because of your platform, but you also know by doing it yourself you get to keep an additional 80-90 percent of the revenue. The opportunity cost doesn't justify giving up that percentage of revenue from your book in exchange for the design, editing, and distribution a publisher provides, so you will just pay an author-funded publisher to do those tasks for you while you keep 100 percent of the

marketing and sales responsibility for yourself and your team.

The truth in my experience is that sometimes it's a terrific investment to pay to publish and sometimes, it's not. There are good reasons to pay to publish and there are good reasons *not* to pay to publish.

So let's get real ... was it a mistake for Ken to pay to publish all those years ago?

I reached out to him on Facebook recently and asked. "Truth is," he said "I'm not real proud that I didn't find a publisher. I did have an agent. And, after I had an agreement with the agent, I had an offer from a traditional publisher, which I felt honor bound to forgo. It would have been a hotter property if I'd have included juicy gossip. Which I could've done; I chose not to do so. Truthfully, today there are options – e.g., print on demand – not available then. 20 years later? Who knows? I'd have done some things differently, sure. But I never would have passed on Fithian's offer to publish a story I thought would be worthwhile – albeit as a niche tale – to historians. At that point, the only alternative was letting it rot in a desk drawer or on a floppy disk and that just felt wrong. It was an investment, sure, but I'm still glad I did it."

So to the "You-don't-pay-to-publish" crowd … I hear you. I get the message and I believe it – for you. But for some people, some of the time, paying to publish is just about the smartest thing you can do.

I've got no horse in this race, except to honor all of the empowered choices the hundreds of authors I have worked with over the years have made.

I've had authors self-publish with success.

I've had authors pay to publish with success.

I've had authors give up 90 percent of their revenue to a traditional publisher with success.

I support them all if these decisions are made for the right reasons.

But then I have had authors stick their manuscript in a drawer never to see the light of day. And with those authors, I think about the lives they could have changed, the difference they could have made, and the sense of completion and accomplishment they could have had – and I think: "Wow, what a bummer! You could have made a difference and you chose not to because the path to publishing is hard or confusing or maybe because you were afraid of your own greatness."

That's just not a choice I can support.

So pay, don't pay, give away your revenue to a traditional publisher – whatever! In my book – as long as you are putting it out there to make a difference and help people and not hiding your light – it's a win. But if you want to get a book out there while you build the platform it takes for a publisher to take a risk on you, you are going to need to look at self-publishing and hybrid publishing options which may, in fact, require you to have some skin in the game. So that's what we are going to cover next.

CHAPTER FIVE

Should I Self-Publish?

One of my first jobs after college was doing research for authors and one of the first books I worked on was about lottery winners. The book had eighty stories of lottery winners, a bunch of whom I had the opportunity to interview in preparation for the book. These were all people who had won $1,000,000 or more after taxes in the 1980s and 1990s in the US.

Of the people featured in the book, there were three lottery winners, of the eighty, who already had considerable wealth and already had a personal wealth manager before they won. For these people, the money had virtually no effect on their life except to speed up retirement plans. But of the other seventy-seven winners who went from rags to riches almost overnight, the money dramatically affected them as they spent it all and then lost it all (plus some) generally in a matter of three to five years.

I was in my early 20s when I interviewed those lottery winners and I instantly connected their experience with money to my experience with weight. I had just gone from 243 lbs. to 167 lbs. but over the course of my interviews with these people, my weight began to creep up. I was travelling for work to interview them. I wasn't as committed to going to the gym. My strict diet of Jenny Craig boxed food was replaced by failed attempts at portion control. And by the time that book was published, I had ballooned up over 250 lbs. What took me a year to lose, had taken me only a few months to pack back on.

While it may seem unconnected, this germ of an idea – if you aren't ready for success you won't be able to sustain it – is the true secret to self-publishing like a pro.

Most people think there are two ways to publish – either through a traditional publisher or on their own. The truth is self-publishing doesn't mean just one thing. It means a lot of things and in this chapter I'm going to cover as many of them as I can – but the big take-away, not to spoil the surprise, is that whether you get picked up by a traditional publisher or you publish on your own in any way, you must take full control of the process of exploiting your right.

There is no knight coming on a white horse, and even if there were, you wouldn't want that anyway, right? I mean who wants to ride side-saddle on the back of a horse while someone else controls the direction?

My stats might be wrong here – and I'm not going to try to look them up – but my guess is better than 90 percent of people who have a traditional publishing contract who are happy with the outcome have full control of their career. Maybe they have a manager and maybe they don't but they know what they want and they are going for it.

It's easy for us to think – when I get X outcome I will have Y feeling.

When I lose weight, I'll be happy.

When I get the guy, I'll feel loved.

When I score the publishing deal, I'll feel accomplished and proud of myself.

But we have the order of events all wrong. The outcome doesn't cause the feeling, the *feeling* creates the outcome – or something better.

That's why all the people I interviewed for that lottery book lost the money they were so happy to win.

The Problem with Waiting for a Traditional Deal

I've been working with authors since 1994. Some of them have made the *New York Times* Bestseller list and some never finished their book. Want to know the difference between the two? Many people would guess it was the publisher they went with that's the deciding factor, but they would be wrong. The real difference is that authors who understand their business model – and know *why* they are writing and what a completed book will do for them – are always more successful. It's really that simple.

Once you understand *why* you are writing, picking a publisher will come naturally. There is no right or wrong answer. The reason it's confusing (and the book industry is really confusing for first-time authors!) is because the onus is on the author to understand their own business model and pick the publishing method that fits. Many authors, however, don't know where to start so they choose a path without really understanding the option or the consequences!

One of my clients, Julie, was new to writing and to life coaching. She held off building her new coaching practice and instead worked her tail feathers off for two years to get her manuscript accepted by Penguin Books and she was thrilled when it was published. While her advance was small – just $5,000 – she figured with the Penguin name and the quality of her book – plus a celebrity foreword, she'd earn out the advance in no time and have a monthly royalty check that would pay off a new car.

About three months after Julie's book was published, she started to understand what the other publishers who turned her down were talking about. She had sold about 800 books, was frustrated with her publisher for not doing more marketing, her books were no longer in bookstores, and she wished she had never signed with Penguin in the first place. If she had to do it all over again, Julie says she would have self-published the day she finished her manuscript and spent those two years building her business, instead of begging to be published.

My client Lisa was in a similar boat. New to coaching, Lisa put a proposal together and shopped it around. Her vision was clear: she wanted a TV show and this book was the cornerstone to an elaborate national press strategy. When she met with agents and publishers, she explained her goal and said, "I have a proposal here, but I'd like to know what kind of a book sounds interesting to you."

Like Julie, Lisa got a small advance: $3,500. Unlike Julie, Lisa wasn't writing the book of her dreams, instead she was writing a book that her research indicated would make it easy for her to get free publicity. Lisa's goal for this book was to start building her platform and having St. Martin's Press behind her helped with the bookings. It was well worth the eighteen-month wait. Lisa isn't sure how many books she's sold. "It's not very many," she says. But she was recently booked on Good Morning America and quoted in the *New York Times*.

The point of those stories is that every type of publishing has options, but if you don't understand your business strategy – if you don't start out with the end in mind – you'll be likely to be unhappy with your publisher or your book's performance. It won't surprise you to know, this is significantly easier said than done!

Many of my clients are just starting their coaching practices and their goal is to establish their expertise and build their subscriber list. Ultimately this will help them get a major advance with a traditional publisher, but they don't have the time to spend trying to get a publisher or waiting the years it takes to go through the standard process. To short-cut the system, many of my clients work hard to get a book out within a year of opening the doors of their business, either through self-publishing or another alternative, like the one we offer our year-long clients with Difference Press.

There is a thrill to being accepted by a traditional publisher and a credibility bump that is nearly unrivaled. One of the top reasons for pursuing traditional publishing is the desire for validation and legitimacy. This desire shouldn't be minimized. It's important to recognize what percentage of your interest in traditional publishing is to get that validation so you can examine your assumptions about how you can best get the approval you seek.

The Pros and Cons of Traditional Publishing

Pros	Cons
• Advance payment of royalties	• Low profit per book (5-8% royalty is standard)
• Shelf space in brick-and-mortar book stores	• Difficult to get a deal
• Prestige and validation	• Once you sell the book, you lose control over it
• Help with getting reviews	• Very little promotional help (beyond shelf space and review requests)
• Introductions to book editors, proofreaders, and people with marketing experience	• Little incentive to promote the book yourself (since profits per book are generally less than $1.00)
• No worries about design or formatting	• Inflexibility for future editions
• Motivation and accountability	• Deadlines which might not be convenient for you
• Better access to mainstream media and conference speaker circuit	

- Easy to get the book formatted, designed, and printed

- No upfront money required

- Not designed to get clients, instead designed to sell books which benefits publisher most

- No control over cover art, back, spine, press releases, ads, or other media the publisher releases

- Need a platform to get a contract, but if you have a platform, you don't need a contract

Do-It-Yourself Self-Publishing

If you want your primary income to come from the sale of books, writing is a small fraction of your job. You should begin to think of yourself as the owner of a book business whose job tasks include writing, publishing, and marketing. You will wear many hats and one of those hats may include finding an agent and traditionally publishing sometimes.

Here are some of the skills you will need to learn yourself or learn how to hire out.

Editing – Whether you work with a developmental editor or you hire a freelance editor, you will need to work with an objective third party to make sure your manuscript is in its best form before going to print. At Difference Press, we use three types of editors, developmental editors, line editors, and proofreaders. You will need to study different types of editors, decide on which ones you need, and hire the right people.

Art Direction – In any big project like a book, having a single person holding the vision of the look, feel, and branding of your book is essential to having clean, consistent design inside and out. If you are self-publishing, you may end up as your own art director but beware, this role is deceptively difficult, so you must study and learn the skills of great art direction for books.

Cover Design – There is a great deal of science that goes into book cover design. After all, people don't read your book before they buy it – the cover is usually all they have to go on. As a DIY self-publisher, you may find you make your own covers! Many of the "Smarter Artists" do! There are low cost and free templates out there – see Canva as one example – and you can become a designer but keep in mind, your book title and design are the two biggest keys to determining sales – so you will need to become an expert in this area as well or plan to invest here.

Interior Design – Someone needs to pick a type face for the text that is not only readable but fits the style of your book. That person is your interior designer. They'll have other responsibilities too, especially if you have worksheets, or tips. We have two types of interior designers at Difference Press – one for eBooks and one for print books. You will need to learn some of the tools out there like Vellum or Jutoh or Pronoun as well as buying and learning InDesign – or you will need to hire someone to do your interiors. I will say most of the "Smarter-Artist" types have learned to do this on their own so they can make changes quickly.

Production Management – Getting your book printed is a critical step in the process. Someone will need to find the best printer whether it's print on demand or a more traditional approach. Sourcing the paper managing for the printer is all part of production management. Are you awesome at project management? If so, fantastic! You can leverage that as you run your DIY publishing efforts. Getting lots of books out is the key to making a living from writing. I met one self-publishing author who published 50 books last year. That was one per week with two weeks of vacation! You can see how hiring it out just wouldn't make sense for her.

Registration – Your publisher will also provide you with a unique ISBN number to identify your book as well as a Library of Congress Control number to help make it easy for your book to get found. You'll need to learn how to do this – the great news is so many tools out there now make it easy. Start with Bowker (MyIdentifiers.com) for more details.

Planning – A "managing editor" (that's you if you are self-publishing) needs to keep track of the whole project. At Difference Press, we use project management software for this. You might want to check into Basecamp, Trello, or Asana to keep your projects on track.

Distribution – How does the book go from the printer into a customer's hands? Someone is going to need to manage relationships with large and independent bookstores, online book outlets, Baker & Taylor and/or Ingram for ordering, and specialty distribution relationships. Or you can just stick with Amazon. These are the types of decisions the Smart Artists take pride in making. If books aren't just a way to get clients, you have to think first and foremost about how to get paying book buyers or you will be out of business. Distribution is one of your most important jobs – much more important than writing a book!

Selling – Publishers will send catalogs and sales staff to libraries, schools, and bookstores. If you are self-publishing, this step is likely to get skipped unless it's central to your business model. But how will you sell? Putting a plan together, understanding the numbers and running the P&L – that's all on you.

Marketing – Publishers have marketing staffs that send out review copies of your book and in some cases help you plan a book tour. Sadly, those marketing techniques are pretty ineffective. To sell your book, you'll need to build a list of fans online and off. Free publicity is one part of the equation – social media, search engine optimization, and email marketing are a few of the others.

Promotional Copy – One of the many over-looked aspects of book writing is the jacket copy and other short summaries of the books used on Amazon.com or in catalogs. In about 100 words, the promotional copy writer has to sell the book's sizzle. You will also need to spend considerable time on endorsements, reviews, and book blurbs.

Whew! That is seriously a full-time job, right? It's easy to see why traditional publishers think they earn 90 percent of the revenue from your book in exchange for doing all that. The truth is, writing the book probably is just 7-10 percent of the total effort in getting a book out into the world in a meaningful way.

If you are going to make a serious go of being a writer in the twenty-first century, this is the way to do it. Teaching these skills to people is not my sweet spot – but as we discussed in Chapter Four – the "Smarter Artist" crowd has this covered. Check them out. I also love Johanna Penn from The Creative Penn podcast and blog.

The Pros and Cons of Self-Publishing

Pros	Cons
• Royalties close to 100% (though there will be some costs)	• No advance payment
• No approval process; you maintain complete control	• Quality can suffer due to lack of expertise
• Easy and flexible to make updates	• No prestige or 3rd party validation
• In the long run, it's cheaper to pay money upfront and get higher residual profits	• Can be expensive depending on how much you outsource
• You can always do a traditional publishing deal after	• More work than just handing over a manuscript
• No deadlines/ work at your own pace	• No external motivation
• Total control over cover art, back, spine, press releases, ads, paper quality, and everything else	• Bad distribution options if your book targets an older or less tech-savvy audience

- No agent needed

- The time from proposal to "go live" set by you

- Limited opportunities to hit the big print bestseller lists (e.g. *New York Times* Bestseller)

- Takes time to figure out how to prepare, submit, and sell your books online

Author-Funded Publishing: A Reasonable Alternative to Self-Publishing

Self-Publishing, as an alternative to the legacy commercial publishers, is one that has expanded in popularity dramatically over the past five years. Today, there are many successful self-published authors who did not have the wait and struggle associated with traditional publishing. The cost is not insignificant. As a self-publisher, authors work with a company or freelancers to accomplish the same tasks a publisher would tackle over the year or so they'd spend with your manuscript.

Technically, there are many ways to "self-publish." To truly self-publish you'll be responsible for everything from getting the ISBN, to cover design, line editing, interior design, Library of Congress registration, and much more. You can hire people to do each of those pieces separately or hire one person to do all those steps but if the ISBN is in your name – it's self-published. The problem with self-publishing is it requires someone like a life coach to become a marketing and publishing expert on top of their coaching profession.

If that seems like too much work, you can find an author-funded publisher to manage the process of getting your book published and distributed. When you self-publish on your own or with an author-funded publisher, you retain all rights and royalties in exchange for paying up front to have your book published as a service.

Without the checks and balances of a traditional publishing company, a self-published book can often be spotted for its poor design and editing. That's why picking the right author-funded publisher can make the difference between a success and a failure. All the money you spend on the front end can be recouped if your book is done well. As always, it's a balance between risk and reward.

Often people tell me they don't want to self-publish because they don't want to market the book. Sadly, no matter how you publish, you will be responsible for your own marketing. There are very, very few exceptions, even with the traditional houses. It's true when you self-publish, it's unlikely your books will be on bookstore shelves. But it's equally unlikely if you publish commercially that you'll be able to get bookstores to keep your book in stock beyond ninety days of publication. To sell your book, you need to find your audience and write a book that resonates with them. There is no silver bullet.

Self-publishing will enable you to get a book out quickly and to maintain full control and rights. You'll pay for that privilege and it's easy to go wrong, but you can always make changes and adjustments as you learn more – which is not possible with commercially published books.

Understanding the Alternatives to Traditional Publishing or DIY Self-Publishing

Finding a traditional publisher can take months, and once you have a contract, it usually takes 18 months before your book is in your hands.

Self-publishing is scary and filled with details, logistics, and minutia. Authors need to learn the technical and creative aspects of making and selling books and the chance of getting it wrong the first time is pretty high.

The dichotomy in publishing has long been established but in recent years, space has opened up between the professional, traditional publishing industry and the DIY approach of self-publishing. I understand the "You-don't-pay-to-publish" crowd, but man, to me and the authors I work with, the opportunity cost of becoming a DIY publishing expert is very high.

If you have a small platform, and aren't churning a significant profit yet, getting a traditional publishing contract is going to be very hard for you. And if you can get one, like our lottery winners, you are going to be disappointed in the results if it's something you scrounge together.

Over a million manuscripts are written each year, yet less than 3 percent are published commercially. Assume it's going to be an intense two-year process before you see any harvest for your labors. At the end of all that effort, there is a small chance you see a positive return on your investment. The vast majority of traditionally-published books never break even and only a tiny minority ever achieve big success. If you have a platform and are still building your business, it's a big risk to take.

In this regard, self-publishing is often a better option for new authors and coaches, but it's got some big downsides even beyond the investment. It's as easy to waste as much time as you would to pursue a traditional publishing agreement when you are self-publishing. You are in uncharted waters and the fear of making mistakes can be paralyzing. Plus, without a publisher tapping their foot waiting for your manuscript, it's easy to miss your self-imposed deadlines.

This is why I recommend most experts who are using a book to drive coaching, consulting, and speaking businesses, just pay to publish at the beginning.

When you pay to publish, you get the advantage of publishing your book with an established and experienced publishing company and getting your book out in the world quickly. You don't have to invest the time and energy to learn all the details of the publishing industry because you have a publishing partner who's got your back.

It's important for me to mention again, we don't change people to publish at The Author Incubator. I do include free publishing services for my yearlong clients and I'll discuss that in detail in Chapter 7 so you can steal some of the ideas we use with our clients.

My key recommendation here though is to focus first on having a strategic business coach or manager so you really understand what success will look like for your book. Once you have this, how you publish is significantly less relevant. We want to make sure that you KEEP your metaphorical lottery winnings so you want to be like the 3 lottery winners who already knew how to manage their wealth – not like the ones who went crazy spending for a couple years and then lost it all.

I will encourage you to work with your coach or manager to find the right team to pay to do your publishing. There are lots of great options but none of them will hold the vision for your project. That is your job. You must know what success looks like and drive your vendors to meet that success. Don't expect author-funded publishing services to be something they aren't. They are just implementers of tactics – the strategy, must still, very much, be your own.

The Pros & Cons of Author-Funded Publishing

Pros	Cons
• Have a publishing partner with experience to guide you through the process	• Share control of design, timing, and other aspects of publishing
• Higher royalties per book than a traditional publisher (Aim for 100%)	• Author required to place a financial upfront bet on themselves
• 3rd party validation of an independent publisher	• Harder and slower to make updates than DIY approach
• Little work or learning curve about publishing; Just hand over your manuscript and you'll get your book	• No advance payment
	• None of the special in-store display and promotional opportunities exclusive to traditional publishers
• Strict deadlines to provide accountability and external motivation	• Limited opportunities to hit the big print bestseller lists (e.g. *New York Times* Bestseller)
• Distribution deals	

- No agent needed

- Relatively short time from proposal to "go live"

- Higher quality product than DIY (especially at the beginning)

- Timeline not in author's control

- Can be slower than DIY (depending on how good/fast you get)

- Multi-layer approval process

Your Book.
Your Business.
Your Choice.

The way I see it, you've got a choice to make. Until we get traditional publishers begging to publish your book, you can learn the DIY skills of a modern author-business, or you can pay someone to handle those tasks for you. Both options have pros and cons but the one thing that doesn't change between the two options is that you must take full control of your business. You must become the person who has a book that is helping them grow their business. You must decide on what success will feel like and choose to feel that way every day, starting now.

This is why I called my company The Author Incubator and not the Book Incubator. The truth is, it's all about you becoming the person you most want to be. If you need help making that part happen for yourself, Chapters Six and Eight will give you some clues, but don't be shy about it. The key to all of this is simple – to make publishers beg to publish your book, you must be someone worthy of their time, energy, and investment. Start by making yourself someone *you* would beg to work with. Others will follow suit.

CHAPTER SIX

Don't Confuse Selling & Installing

"Don't confuse selling and installing."

I heard this sentence every day for a year before I had any clue what my boss, Todd Frederick, was talking about. Todd is tall, masculine, and prone to wearing Benetton-style rugby shirts that look like they leapt out of a 1990s commercial airing on MTV (back when MTV played music). And back when I knew him, he was a cross between your goofy uncle and the president of that "nice" fraternity when you were back in college.

Todd was the number two guy at AppAssure Software and it wasn't his first rodeo.

He had built and sold another company with the same CEO, Naj Hussain, a few years back. Naj was always the more refined of the two. If Todd looked like a beer drinker, Naj's vibe was Johnny Walker Black ... Reserve. His Adonis-good looks were rare in the Software industry and even though it was a highly male-dominated space, he found a way to leverage his good looks – if only because he was so often photographed with sports cars in racing suits which no self-respecting guy could deny was hella hot.

Todd and Naj knew what it took to create shareholder value. And the answer was steady sales.

At AppAssure, numbers came first.

How much revenue did we need to continue to grow?

To hit that revenue target, how many customers would we need?

To get that many customers, how many sales conversations would we need to have?

To have that many sales conversations, how many leads would we need?

Todd knew the numbers. Cold.

He knew the numbers by the quarter (what our investors cared about), by the month (what our CEO cared about), by the week (what Todd managed us for), and by the day (how he encouraged us to manage ourselves). Frankly, I bet Todd knew the numbers to the hour. If we were falling behind, he could sense it almost before it officially happened and he would course-correct sometimes without us even knowing what was happening. He would add a webinar, tweak a sales script, stagger sales guys' schedules – all in service to the numbers.

We all knew that at some point in the future, the product we were selling – rapid recovery for Windows servers – needed to work and it needed to be good, but ultimately, we could have the best product in the world, and if no one ever bought it, it wouldn't matter.

This is why Todd drilled into my head, "don't confuse selling and installing." And it's why I drill into my author's heads: "No one reads your book *before* they buy it."

What Todd and I mean is that if you can't find anyone to buy it now – even before it's "done" – you won't be able to find someone to buy it later and you will be out of business.

In the case of software, it's one thing to sell the software and another thing to install it in the user's environment and get it working.

To sell the software, you have to share the promise of the problem it will solve and take money from people who have that problem. We call that closing a sale. AppAssure solved a big problem in a way that was faster, better, and cheaper than any other alternative on the market; so Todd knew he could close sales.

To install the software was another matter. Our software worked when it was the only thing running and the machines were at a certain standard. But in the real world, people had all different generations of hardware and software, often cobbled together. It wasn't always as easy to get the software installed in a client environment and get it to work seamlessly as it was in our testing lab.

The good news for Todd was: no installation was required for the sale to close.

This is true of books, too. Your book is only going to be read *after* it's sold. And just like with software, nothing actually will happen with your ideas until after the sale. In the world of books, "installing" includes the book, but it also includes the products and services you sell related to the book. This is how you will address the diverse needs of the different client environments.

Selling is one process.

Installing is another.

Same with books.

Selling is about getting people to agree to let you help them solve their problem.

Installing is about actually solving it.

These are two distinct processes that require different skills and strategies.

Mixing them up is not useful to your movement, your business, or, most importantly, the people you are here to help.

In other words, "Don't confuse selling and installing!" Five words that, if you master them, will change the game for you.

But it's so easy, when the sales guys couldn't close a sale they wanted, to blame the technology or the client. You will want to do the same. You might start to think you need more certifications or you might think all the prospects coming to you are "bad leads."

When you can separate selling from installing, these problems go away.

At AppAssure it would have been easy to get bogged down in the challenges of installing the software in the wild and forget about all the people who needed our help and to lose track of what it was going to take to build the Rapid Recovery movement. But Todd wouldn't let us. That's what makes him such a great leader.

He made us focus on the numbers, called key performance indicators, instead.

1900 leads yielded...

475 sales conversations which progressed to...

190 product demos which generated...

47 clients at $5K a month which grossed...

$235K for the month. (And next month let's ramp it up!)

Naj, understandably the face of the company, would then brag to the press that it was our 4th, 5th, 6th, 7th straight quarter of growth – but the truth was that growth was pre-determined and inevitable. The business was driven by the numbers. It *had* to succeed.

You Will Fund What You Are Passionate about

Now, I love backing up a Windows server as much as the next New-Age, Self-Help junkie out there, but let's just say, it wasn't exactly my life's greatest passion.

Naj and Todd were two of the best business mentors of my life and let me tell you they are *seriously* passionate about Microsoft products and Network Operations. I mean *seriously*! And I am so grateful for them both and all they taught me, but I didn't want to spend my life talking about Cloud storage and Back Up recovery. (Even as I typed that I had a tiny bit of Corporate PTSD Syndrome.)

As passionate as Naj and Todd were about cloud-based architecture and building seamless and robust next generation recovery systems, I was passionate about personal growth.

I spent my time thinking about the idea that only love is real, that life is a projection of our thoughts, that we can bio-hack our bodies and neuro-sculpt our brains, that we can attract romance greater than anything we have ever known, that we can magnetize wealth and abundance beyond our greatest dreams, and that we can construct a future for our planet where learning through joy is privileged over learning through pain.

I watched how Naj and Todd built the Rapid Recovery movement inside the crowded and conservative software-as-a-service industry, and I realized the model they were using could help life coaches and experts build and grow their own movements.

But to do that, I had to convince these non-marketing-oriented professionals to stop confusing "selling and installing."

I knew that was going to be a hard sell.

I watched how Todd had to drill that into every employee's head several times a day and still most people didn't get it. They wanted the answer to be to focus on the product and that by spending lots of time and money building a great product that *then* all the customers would magically come.

The truth was if we waited to have the perfect product, we would be out of business.

Naj and Todd were careful about bringing on investors who might push the business in ways they didn't want to go or might dilute their stake, so they needed consistent revenue from customers.

They couldn't afford to spend more on product development than customers could support. They needed to *fund* their Rapid Recovery *Movement* by making more money than they needed to spend (or at least the same amount).

Instead of focusing on building the best product, they built a "good enough" product at first and sold it. Then they would get feedback from early customers about things that didn't work and just fix those things, instead of building rocket ships to the moon that no one needed. (Which, if you know software developers, is sometimes what they want to do.)

What's This Got to Do with Your Book?

Okay, you are starting to wonder what this has to do with your book. I get it and I appreciate you hanging with me because this is important, and if you get the lesson of this chapter it will have a ripple effect that changes thousands – maybe millions of lives.

Most authors and publishers believe the way to sell more books is to write better books.

They are confusing selling and installing.

The truth is, "No one reads your book before they buy it."

And yes, there is a point at which viral growth and referrals *will* be important – but we are not there yet! First, we need to generate revenue, fund our movement, and get market validation for the product we want to sell.

I mentioned in Chapter Three that we don't charge authors to publish with us. But there is a reason why I do that. It's because I want the entire publishing industry to understand that they are confusing selling and installing, and to do that I need an overwhelming pile of indisputable evidence.

Naj and Todd flipped the software selling process from:

Old way:

Spend lots of time and money to build a great product and then try to sell it and hope you get lucky.

To

New way:

Build a viable product, sell it, and use the revenue to optimize it after it's a sure thing.

I wanted to prove the same is possible for books.

Old way:

Spend lots of time and money to write a book, and then try to sell it and hope you get lucky.

To

New way:

Write a book that is "good enough" to help at least one person solve a real problem, give away the book, but sell the solution to the problem, use the revenue from that sale to optimize to make your product better and to fund the growth of your movement.

Flip the Funnel

This approach is truly flipping the funnel and there was no way I could prove this with folks who just wanted to publish their books. I needed to work with people who wanted to build successful businesses and movements like AppAssure.

This is why I only publish authors who make a one-year (or more) commitment to learning this type of Growth Hack Marketing for Authors.

Look, I know I'm pretty good at marketing and even as a Chief Marketing Officer making

$200,000 a year plus bonuses, it took me almost a year to understand what Todd meant by "Don't confuse selling and installing."

For authors who aren't down with growth hacking, I am happy to teach them to self-publish, to help them find an agent, or to match them with author-funded publishing services. But for authors who want to go on the growth-hacking ride with me, I am happy to provide free publishing services and let them keep all their book revenue, so long as my authors are willing to help me create a mountain of evidence for this new model of publishing – where the book is not a point fixed in time, but rather, an evolving organism with versions and releases much like software.

In essence, my clients are co-creators of my product and members of my movement.

In the next chapter, I'm going to explain how my unorthodox method of publishing works. Again, you can't *buy* this service. It's not for sale. But you can copy it. And I encourage you to do just that.

CHAPTER SEVEN

The Difference Press Experiment

On June 12, 2014, Elon Musk released all the Tesla patents with a promise not to sue anyone for using them. Musk wasn't totally benevolent here. He just recognized that patents frequently hold back and limit innovation, especially around core infrastructure.

I'm doing the same thing. Yes, The Difference Process is trademarked and still I'd love it if this idea inspires you and how you publish.
By all means, credit me for helping you in your thinking – but the truth is, I can't change the 200-year-old publishing industry on my own.

I need you to put these ideas into action even if you aren't a part of The Author Incubator family.

If you *get* this, then I want you to "steal like an artist" and run with this model. You don't have to work with me. I am giving it all away right here. Yes, this is included for authors who commit to becoming growth hackers and working with me to get their movements funded through product and services sales – but this isn't rocket science – it's just innovation.

There is No English Teacher in the Sky Judging Your Book

So how does it work?

First, you have to remember that we aren't trying to write a "*good*" book by some objective standard. Just like AppAssure wasn't trying to build "*good*" software. We don't want to focus on writing a "*good*" book. We need to write a "*good enough*" book.

There is no English teacher in the sky who splits books up between the "good ones" (presumably

War & Peace, The Catcher in the Rye, and *Great Gatsby*) and the "not good ones" (all the books we have never heard of). There are many books which are better than *War & Peace* that have never seen the light of day and therefore they can't make the difference they were born to make.

I am redefining "good book" as a book that can get into someone's hands, change their heart, and ultimately bring hope, healing, and transformation to their life.

Now listen, a three-page book with an average of sixteen typos per page and no new ideas *can't* change someone's life. So, there is a *bare minimum* required. I call that bare minimum the "table stakes" – required for a book that makes a difference.

- You have to have a powerful message of hope, healing, and transformation.
- You need to be able to share that message in a way that is organized enough for at least some people to follow (I just want you to start by finding ten people who can follow it.)

- You need to write it in a way that the typos and grammatical errors aren't so distracting that your reader missed the points.

That's it – those are the minimum requirements you must bring to the table – a good idea that actually works, written in a way that is logical and legible.

And here is the real kicker ... I don't want you to do much more than that. Why? Well because if you spend decades trying to write the Great American Novel (or the Great British Novel, or Great Australian Novel) it's going to be so much harder for you to pivot when no one is buying what you are selling.

The magic of AppAssure was that the product grew and changed with the clients. The developers didn't spend years creating a product that no one bought, they spent days creating a skeleton they could partner with early adopters to shape into something magical. Doesn't that sound fun? I know it is for me!

You will need a book that's good enough, sure.

But there is no English teacher in the sky that is going to determine if it's good enough based on how you turn a phrase. The arbiter is the audience.

Once we have the idea for the book, we can start testing the message. Before our authors write even one word on the page I want them to sell at least ten clients into the program they will sell to readers who like the message of the book the most.

Ten clients at a minimum sales price of $1,000 is $10,000 to *fund their movement*.

Start with Revenue that Funds Your Movement

I want you to start with revenue not because I care about money, but because there is no way to change the planet without it.

A good book alone can't fund your self-care.

A good book alone can't fund a place for you to host readers for discussions.

A good book alone can't fund professional videos that can reach around the world.

A good book alone can't do any of that.

You need early adopters to partner with to grow your movement. Your early adopters will fund you not by giving you charity, but by paying you to solve painful problems they have. This will make them not only funders of your movement, but evangelists of it.

As you deliver more hope and healing, the universe will start to recognize you as a steward of abundance and because you are a safe place for money to flow, more and more will flow to you in proportion to the amount of change you are making on the planet.

Here's How You Start

Step 1. Come up with an idea for a book that solves a problem.

Step 2. Test the idea by selling a permanent solution to the problem.

Step 3. Partner with your early adopters (we call them beta clients in my program) to shape the book and the program simultaneously.

Step 4. Release Version 1 of your book as an *eBook* only.

Inside The Author Incubator, our authors spend about nine weeks developing an idea, testing it in the marketplace, and writing their draft manuscript in partnership with those early adopters.

Once the manuscript is written, they are invited to edit and publish the manuscript on their own, with a traditional publisher, or if they want to join my growth hacking movement, with us.

It's a huge risk to publish with us because you give up control over your process and you don't get the big name recognition of going with a Big 5 publisher, but many of our clients have made so much progress in those nine weeks, they decide to take the risk and I'm grateful for and humbled by that decision when it happens.

At this point we have:

- A manuscript (largely unedited)
- A title
- A book description
- A program we are selling to people interested in the book
- Early adopter clients

From that point, we embark together on a one-year journey, where each quarter we are growing and expanding the movement.

Q1 for Your Book

The first thing we do (and what I am recommending for you), is set a publishing deadline sixty days from completion of the manuscript. This is the maximum time I recommend. I base a lot of my thinking and planning on the agile software development process here but we are going to do several mini releases of our "product" (a.k.a. the book) and then we are going to put the eBook or the beta version of the software out to the marketplace quickly to get feedback before we develop too much.

Here's the timeline I recommend to get your eBook out. Remember it doesn't have to be perfect. In fact it can't and won't be perfect – that's an impossible and self-defeating standard and one that smacks of confusing selling and installing.

Here's what your agile development plan looks like for Q1 of your book project.

- Line edit of the manuscript – two weeks
- Proofreading of the manuscript – two weeks
- Cover design & interior layout for eBook – two weeks
- Prep for launch – two weeks
- Release and gather feedback – two weeks
- Make changes to eBook based on feedback – two weeks

By focusing on each step along the way for just a couple of weeks, you can minimize the work load and stay focused on getting it "good enough" to ship (as Seth Godin would say).

We have a super fun eBook release process which is part direct response marketing and part Law of Attraction. If you are using this model for your own launch, here's what I recommend.

First, get together about ten people to support your launch. The way we do it, we get ten authors together to co-promote each other's books. Plan a specific launch day and focus all your effort on this day. The launch day itself is your Law of Attraction moment to bask in gratitude for what you have accomplished. Everything leading *up* to that launch day is how you generate revenue. Each two-week milestone is an opportunity to share your progress and generate leads and referrals. If these milestones aren't leading to clients, refine your message. Don't wait until the book is done. Each part of the process is a chance to co-create the book with your readers and future readers.

By the time your eBook comes out, my goal for our authors is for them to generate $10,000 in revenue. This tells us you are headed in a direction that has market validation.

Q2 for Your Book

Once your eBook is out and the changes have been incorporated, I don't want you to think of the project as *done* (which is what most people who have a publisher, self-publish, or pay to publish do when their book is released). Instead I want you to think of it as your second round of feedback.

You got your first round of feedback before the publishing process started while you were writing your manuscript. The second round came when you were editing and publishing your eBook. If you were able to generate $10,000 before you finished publishing your eBook, you are getting a huge thumbs-up from the universe that your messaging is *on point*! Keep going.

If you didn't, this next phase is all about iterating and optimizing. We need to hit that first $10K goal. Then we need a $10K a month goal. And then we will work to double that. By the end of the year, if you are able to have a $25K or $30K month, we will know your movement is funded and we are ready to move forward. If not, we decide if we are going to continue to invest in this movement based on the empirical evidence.

The second quarter of your book's life is all about getting pre-orders of your print book. Now remember, at this point the eBook is live and the changes to your manuscript have been made so you are ready to go to print. You should have clients, early readers, and reviews to leverage for the next milestone.

The first thing to do at this stage is to create a free book preorder offer & start giving away your print book (you can charge for shipping). When someone signs up, offer them a free call with you to assess what is going on with them and see if you can help even before your book comes out. Explain that if they are having a problem you know how to solve, you don't want them to wait until your pre-order launch day.

You've got ninety days to get your print book done and to get 100 pre-orders of your book. Here's what your agile development plan looks like for Q2 of your book project.

- Create free book offer page and set launch date – two weeks
- Get interior designer layout interior – two weeks
- Design for spine and back cover – two weeks
- Set price and upload to print on demand service – two weeks
- Print proofing process – two weeks
- Launch print books – two weeks

During Q2, you should be able to generate at least $20,000. (I'd like to see it closer to $30,000 for this quarter to know we have continued market validation.)

Remember, publishing is secondary. Don't confuse selling and installing! Yes, we need a "good enough" print book – but if we can't fund your movement with sales, we have to adjust the messaging now! Not later!

If you can give away 100 copies of your book as a part of your free book funnel, you should be able to get another twenty-five clients from that pool through direct outreach.

Q3 for Your Book

Q3 is all about playing with scale. You have gotten your first ten-thirty clients through hand-to-hand combat. At The Author Incubator we call this "Direct Outreach" but now you have to start reaching out to Other People's Audiences through advertising, sponsored speaking, or other direct response marketing techniques in order to see if this baby can scale. We want Q3 to generate at *least* $30,000 in sales – but now we want to start playing with balancing direct outreach, referrals, and fresh traffic from other sources.

Here's what your Q3 might look like once you have the author copies of your book:

- Create advertising campaign to free book offer – two weeks
- Create auto-responders to increase conversions – two weeks
- Optimize advertising for the launch – two weeks
- Optimize landing page – two weeks

- Make final changes to manuscript, cover, and marketing copy – two weeks
- Make changes to eBook – two weeks

Q3 is all about locking down what is working. You need to know your key performance indicators and how to move the levers. If you get this right, Q3 will be a $30K quarter for you, heading toward our six-figure year.

Q4 for Your Book

Stage four – Books in bookstores

Shakespeare says in the play Hamlet "The readiness is all." And it's as true with your book project as it was with the play Hamlet put on to try to "catch the conscience of the king." You are trying to catch the conscience of the reader. If your book hasn't hooked readers who want to co-fund your movement and build your revolution with you, this is the quarter to find out if it's possible. If you haven't done it in a year, that's okay if there are signs you are headed in the right direction, but you need to be able to make a compelling case you can get there if you can't do it by the end of this quarter. You have ninety days left. Our *minimum* goal is $10K a month in revenue that comes from your book. Ideally, I'd love you to have a $25K month in this final quarter. We want between $40K and $60K of revenue in these last ninety days.

You should have your advertising running or some way to get consistent new leads. You should know how many leads you need to hit your revenue goal and you should know how and where to get those leads.

Here's what your Q4 might look as you get your books into bookstores:

- Print and eBooks live on Amazon – two weeks
- Launch party with sponsors and sponsorships – two weeks
- Launch back end or upsell program to accelerate sales – two weeks
- Increase ad spend based on conversions – two weeks

- Final analysis of campaign to date – two weeks
- Hire up or wind down project – two weeks

For our authors, within a year (plus the nine weeks or so it takes to write the book) we know if we have a winner and hopefully we are neutral or positive from a revenue perspective to find that out. (Even losing ideas can recoup losses with this growth hacking approach.)

What success looks like to me is $100K in revenue from your book (not book sales, but business that comes through the book) within twelve months of the eBook release. If we can't get there in a year – or at least to a couple consecutive $10K months near the end of that journey – this is probably not the best use of your energy. It's a sign you are not doing your highest work on the planet.

Now, to assess that, you have to actually work a plan hard for a year to find out. If you can't make that commitment, in my opinion, you just have a lottery ticket. And that's cool – roll the dice, see what happens, assume it will be nothing but hey one in a million hit – maybe that will be you.

Recap for Readers

If you aren't the gambling type and you want to do something you know will work, these are the Difference Press Book Launch stages.

Pre-Stage 1 – Build Launch Team – folks who sign up to get the book for free (if you can't give it away, you can't sell it!)

Stage 1 – Soft Launch of EBook Only (keep the price low) - $10K

Stage 2 – Pre-orders of print book (free plus shipping funnel to cover your cost) - $20K

Stage 3 – Print book launch (author copies) - $30K

Stage 4 – Books in bookstores - $40K

Total one-year revenue goal: $100K

Hey, That Reminds Me!
Failure Is Not an Option

Remember how I told you in the last chapter how my boss, Todd Frederick, was often correcting course of our sales and marketing team by the hour? That's how well you should know your numbers so success is inevitable.

There was another thing Todd used to say. And I thought it was a little Star-Trek-cheesy-successy sort of statement but now I get it.

At least once a day, Todd would say, "Failure is not an option."

I kinda thought that was naïve and a tad irritating. Of course, failure is an option – I don't like it, but that is the fact! Right?

Wrong! What I have come to realize with the perspective of time is that failure really wasn't an option because Todd didn't hold space for failure. Like ever. From anyone. For even a second.

That's what I focus on most with my clients – creating an environment where, in true fact, failure just isn't an option. We put the metrics in place. We act as if. We trust the process. We follow through. This process simply can't fail.

Now when you compare that to the lottery approach the traditional publishing industry takes from the last chapter, maybe you can see why I am so passionate about changing the entire publishing industry.

It is actually 100 percent possible to live in a world as a non-fiction author where *Failure Is Not an Option*. Crazy as the publishing industry would have you believe it is, this is a real, viable option.

AppAssure, by the way, was sold to Dell for an undisclosed amount of (a heck of a lot) of millions of dollars. Failure really wasn't an option. And it doesn't have to be for you, either. I promise.

CHAPTER EIGHT

Growth Hacks for Non-Fiction Authors

This book is about what it takes to get publishers begging to work with you. And more than that, it's about the feeling and the results that you want for your book and your business. You may have started this book thinking a book was a path to passive income revenue.

Typically, here's what my authors think their book journey will look like:

1. Come up with an amazing idea for a book.
2. Based on the quality of the writing, get picked up by a top five publisher.

3. Collect a $100,000 book advance to pay living expenses while spending a year in a cabin in Asheville, North Carolina writing the next *Eat, Pray, Love.*

4. Hand the book to the publisher and have them do all the marketing.

5. Get featured on the *Today* show thanks to the publisher getting that deal.

6. Receive monthly royalty checks of $5,000 - $10,000 from book sales (starting almost immediately).

7. Occasionally, do a retreat somewhere exotic for a little extra cash and because readers are begging for it.

THIS DOES NOT HAPPEN! YOU MUST UNDERSTAND THIS IN NO UNCERTAIN TERMS!

Here's what a typical book journey actually looks like:

1. Come up with a book idea.
2. Write it.
3. Get rejected by a bunch of publishers and agents.

4. Self-publish and see how the quality of the work carries it despite not having a big name publisher.
5. Celebrate launch day with a bunch of emails and Facebook posts.
6. Scratch head about why you're not getting sales.
7. Decide books don't work for you.

My purpose in this book is for you to understand this process doesn't have to be a new casino game. There is no magic that comes from a traditional deal. The magic comes from you.

Here's a typical #incubatedauthor book journey:

1. Come up with a few ideas for books.
2. Put out an MVP (minimum viable product) to test the book ideas.
3. Get a few new "beta" clients and collect a few thousand dollars in revenue to validate the idea.
4. Use the time with "beta" clients to write the book.

5. Use the process of writing the book to test concepts, titles, and covers. Each successful test should lead to more market validation – which includes clients and revenue.

6. Generate at least $10,000 to be able to put into publishing and marketing your book in a way that allows you to make a killer investment in yourself.

7. Use the book launch to generate more clients at twice the rate you were charging while you were writing books.

8. Get great results from your clients and have them give copies of your book to their friends, creating a self-perpetuating referral engine.

9. Forget to look at book royalties for a year and then realize you have made enough money from book sales to surprise your family with a trip to Disney world.

10. Enjoy repeatable five- to six-figure months and then write your next book to take your movement to the next wider concentric circle out.

This does *not* have to be a gamble. This is a repeatable process that works every single time – by definition. You don't write the book until you have the market validation that the book idea will lead to the outcome you want!
You *sell* the book before you write it!

I call this growth hacking for authors.

Growth hacking comes from the venture-capital-funded start-up world. Remember when I told you about my experience working at that company called AppAssure? Well, that company was about the tenth VC-funded company I ran the marketing for. My specialty was using online media buying of paid search, SEO, affiliate and display advertising and content marketing (mostly books and blogs) to provide a steady, repeatable flow of leads to sales teams or sales pages.

Flip Your Funnel

For my high-ticket clients, like AppAssure, the leads went to sales teams who would then close the sales. For my low-ticket and subscription clients, like Identity Guard, we would drive traffic to a webpage to close sales.

Here is how the funnel worked at AppAssure:

Ad buys on Google and other places would lead prospects to download a free copy of our book. The people who downloaded the book would receive a series of emails that included case studies and other tips, and within the series, the prospect would be invited to a live product demo. To register for the demo, they had to provide an email. Someone on the sales team would arrange a time to call them and give them a demo. One in eight sales closed. The average sale was $5,000. Our budget was $1,000 per client. Since 1:8 prospects would close, I could spend $125 to get someone to sign up for a demo. Now I knew only one in twenty of the people who downloaded the book would sign up for the demo (even with my email harassing schedule) so that gave me $6 that I could spend to get someone to take my book for free. I like to be an overachiever so I set my goal at $5 per "lead" (or book downloader).

If you are reading correctly, you see I've flipped the funnel. I don't think of books as a *profit* center, I think of them as a marketing *cost*. I don't think of people paying *me* for a book, I think of me investing to get downloads.

Now can you see how easy it is to spend $1 when I know within thirty days I'm going to get $5 back for that investment? For every $1,000 I could spend in advertising, I knew I would end up with 167 email addresses, eight demos, one client, $5,000 in gross revenue. If Todd said we need twenty clients this month, I could say great, I just need $20,000 and I can make that happen.

Can you see how different your life and your business would be with this model?

Or let's look at low-ticket/subscription models. Identity Guard provided identity theft solutions. We had a book called *Bankrupt at Birth* which was about child identity theft. The Identity Guard service was about $20 a month with an average lifetime value of a client at $150.

We were willing to spend $50 to get a client. We would buy ads about child identity theft offering parents a free copy of the book. Once they accepted the book, we presented a thank-you page that allowed them to add on a free seven-day trial of the software. We knew 50 percent of people who took the trial would generate $150 for us. That means we could afford to spend $25 to get someone to sign up for the trial. We had a 20% conversion rate from the thank-you page which meant I had a budget of $5 to get someone to take the free book.

If I had a budget of $50 per client, I would spend $5 to get 10 book downloads. Of those 30 people who downloaded the book, two would sign up for a free trial and one of those would become a client. For every $50 I spent, I would reliably get one new client.

Again in this model I *spend* $5 to give someone the book and to establish my credibility. By the way, working with a traditional publisher is going to make it almost impossible to use your book to generate revenue reliably like this, so until you have a steady flow of cash in your business, you want to make sure you don't rush a traditional publishing deal that ties your hands and makes it impossible for you to spend $5 to give your book away.

In the examples I shared, we were either giving away PDFs of eBooks, or we were charging the client shipping costs for the print book. In my business today, I often pay for shipping myself in offers like this which, of course, decreases the budget you have available to spend.

This is what I call *flipping the funnel*.

Books aren't about generating revenue directly – they are most effective to establish credibility and value to generate a steady flow of leads which you convert into clients. If you are using a book this way, you can see how quickly paying to publish can become cost-effective.

You can also see how if you are thinking of books as a way to generate revenue directly, learning how to become a master of self-publishing would be an essential way to save costs and increase profit margins.

Growth hacking for authors is a way to put the focus on making an actual difference – not just giving 100 or 1,000 or 1,000,000 readers an idea or two; but instead putting all your passion into building a scalable, repeatable business that allows you to fully serve a handful of people a month to completion. Growth hacking is a mindset with which you approach problems.

"The end goal of every growth hacker is to build a *self-perpetuating marketing machine* that reaches millions by itself; however, growth hacking is a process, not a secret book of ideas."
– Aaron Ginn

Steps to Growth Hacking for Authors

Choosing your book topic is one of the most important steps in the process of writing a book that leads to clients. Get this one wrong and there is no amount of marketing that can make up for it. There is no editor you can hire who can or will change your topic. There is no cover designer who can solve a badly chosen book topic with a great design. No amount of marketing can get a book with a badly chosen topic into enough hands to make the difference the author wants it to make. You can't invest your way out of it. The short answer is that more than 50 percent of your success is determined by how well you choose your topic.

Know what you want to get out of your book. Many people feel called to write a book but they aren't sure what they want from the experience. They tell me they want to have written a book – but why? Let's say you wrote a book, it was published, and not a single other human ever read it. Would that be enough? For a few of our clients the answer is yes – but very, very few! Most people want to write a book for it to be read. But wanting it to be read isn't enough unless you are really into playing the lottery. Yes, some books get magically discovered, but the great majority don't. So the way those authors get their books into people's hands is with something called a "back-end" on their books. Your back-end is how you will fund getting your message out to the world. That means you need to know how you will generate the revenue to promote your book *before* you write it. Generally, this is with speaking, coaching, consulting, teaching, or through donations. If you try to write a book that does all of those things, your efforts will be diffused and you will likely succeed at none of them. If you focus your energy on getting a book to do one thing for you, you actually get many other side benefits. The clarity of your intention for your book is essential to picking your topic. If you don't know why you are writing a book, you will almost certainly pick the wrong topic.

Understand the delta between your ideal reader's dream come true and your message. You have a message – whether your book is fiction or non-fiction there is a way you want your reader to be different at the end of the book. And this is important – we must change the reader in this way for the book to serve you. BUT your reader almost certainly doesn't KNOW they want or need this message. If they did, they would already have it, and they wouldn't need the book. More than 50% of the authors-in-transformation who apply to work with us want to write a book about self-love for women in transition. Do you know what's true about women in transition who need self-love? They often don't recognize they are in "transition" (they probably call it something like "I need to get a new job before I get fired!" or "Should I divorce my husband or give him one more ultimatum?") and they *definitely*, 100 percent do not think they need self-love. They think they need a kick in the ass, more instruction, good luck, clarity, guidance, or wisdom – none of which you can receive without self-love, but try convincing them of that!

Practically, what this means is that the only people searching for self-love for women in transition are women who have come to discover they are in transition and need self-love – those are people for whom your book wouldn't be much help and from whom you can't expect a backend sale (more on that later). So there is a gap between what your ideal reader *thinks* she wants and what you know she needs. Your book topic must close that gap. You must sell her what she wants and then give her what she needs.

Drop your ego and lead with service. I know you want to help people and I know this comes from your heart. But the truth is, the way most people attempt to serve is by trying to cram messages they *know* will help and serve their ideal reader down their throats. Remember when your mom used to nag you to put your clothes away so they would be easier to find? She was right. But did that make you do it? Probably not! Telling people they are wrong doesn't tend to inspire action – at least not lasting action. When you tell someone they are "enough" when they don't believe they are, they don't change. When you tell someone they should "love themselves" more when they don't – this isn't service. It might serve you. You might feel very smart and powerful sharing this message. But real service gets through, and for a message to get through, you must first meet people where they are. Let them have their problem the way they see it. If they think they aren't good enough or worthy of love, this will be hard for you. That is the *sacrifice* of service. It's easy for you and satisfying for your ego to tell them they are wrong, but you have to earn that. And you earn that by making the sacrifice of acknowledging and validating how real their problem – the way they frame it – seems to them. Warning: This is *much* harder than it sounds.

Never, ever, ever ask anyone who isn't paying you what they think for the purpose of finding out what *they think*. Many people think the best way to get feedback is by asking. I hear this tragic advice all the time. The truth is people are incapable of giving accurate feedback. I did a PhD and in the process of doing original research for my dissertation, I learned, and validated, that you always bias your own research. When you ask people "Do you think this is a good book topic?" they are incapable of answering that. Instead, they mirror your energy, they satisfy their own ego, they share theoretical opinions based in part on your race or gender or hair color. You know how you know if you have a good book topic? If people buy it (more coming on that). For now, promise me this. Don't ask another living soul what they think about your opinion for the purpose of finding out their opinion. Ask because you want to share your news or get engagement. Ask because you want to make them feel included. Ask because it's nice to ask and be asked. But don't ask because their opinion is valid. It isn't and it will throw you off the scent.

Create an MVP. A few years back a guy named Eric Reis wrote a book called *The Lean Start Up*. You probably haven't read it, but you probably should. I have to give that book a lot of credit for my success. What Eric explained (in reference to technology businesses, but it works even better for service businesses like coaching) was that you can't survey customers to find out what features they want. You have to create and offer "starter" products and see what they use and buy. He calls this a minimum viable product or an MVP. Let's say you want to write a book about why all entrepreneurs should have a dog. You have your topic all sorted. Want to know if it will work? Create an MVP! Create a landing page and offer a thirty-minute call. "Considering getting a dog? Spend thirty minutes with me and we'll review the six essential reasons every entrepreneur should get a dog. You'll find out which breeds are best. Whether a puppy is for you. And how to know you are picking the right dog for you. Register now and if you can't come to the call live, I'll send you the recording." Now – you don't have to write a book to share thirty minutes of info about dogs. You can put this offer out *right now* just in email or Facebook for no charge. If no one signs up for your free call (your MVP), you have not picked the right idea for your book! Before you create your book – create an MVP that gets 100 opt-ins. If you can do that – you are well on your way to choosing a good book topic. This is about 100 percent times more effective than asking people their opinion and what's amazing is it actually doesn't take that much longer to do!

Sell it before you create it. Great news! You don't have to write a book to sell it! Many of our authors fund my mentorship with a Kickstarter or other crowd-funded campaigns. They do this by getting a "working title" and "advance reader cover" and making their book available for pre-order before they have even written a word. Point of fact, many traditional publishers do this too, presenting sample book covers to book buyers and testing the waters before they print 20,000 or 30,000 books. One of the best parts of a crowd-funding campaign is that you have an early base of fans to help you market your book. Yes, you might make some money – we have authors who have generated more than $40,000 to help support their book-marketing and platform-building efforts – but it's not really about the money. The biggest value is building your tribe. If you can't get anyone to buy the book before it's released, you won't get anyone to buy your book after. There is no better way to test a book topic than with a crowd-funding campaign. Now, keep in mind, if you reach your funding goal, you do need to actually write the book! If not, you can move on to the next idea, no harm done.

Create and test the *back end* before you build the front end. Back in points #1 & #2, I mentioned that you want to know the outcome and understand your back-end sales metrics before you write your book. Practically, what this means for most of my clients is that they will use their books to get clients or paid speaking engagements. There is an irony to this, because if you want a book to get clients or speaking engagements, you need to have at least three paid clients or paid speaking engagements in order to write the right book. Once you book three paid clients or three paid speaking gigs, you will know *so* much more about what you want your book to do for you. You'll know if you like working with clients or speaking. You'll know how you have to sell it. You'll know if it's what you want to spend a year doing. And most importantly, you will know exactly what needs to be included in the book in order to maximize sales from readers. Now, getting three paid clients or three paid speaking gigs *without* a book is considerably harder than doing it with a book – but it is possible and it's worth investing in making it happen. You don't want to pick a topic that doesn't lead to a back end because most books just don't make enough money to make that worth it. In order to maximize your book you want to understand how you will use it to grow your business after it comes out. For instance, before I wrote my book *The Difference* I had about ten clients a quarter. After I wrote the book, I was able to generate enough leads to have ten clients a month. I quadrupled my business with a book – but if I hadn't sold my program first, I wouldn't have written the right book.

Think of your book as a love letter to one person. Imagine it's the night before your wedding day and you sit down to write your future husband the love letter to end all love letters. It's sixteen pages. Written in calligraphy. Includes two original poems by you and one you had commissioned personally for him by Mary Oliver.

It's quite possible this love letter will go down in world history. When it's all finished you carefully fold the parchment into thirds and go to put it in the envelope you selected from the custom paper store.... But it's too big! You rush to the kitchen and find a Robin's Egg blue Publisher's Clearinghouse mailer and rip it open, you tuck the letter inside with the parchment showing through the little velum address window. You tape up the envelope and leave it in a pile with the other junk mail and circulars.

Will your betrothed ever get this letter? *No*! Not very likely.

When you pick the wrong topic for your book, your ideal reader never finds it. You must have the right-sized envelope and write their name beautifully on the cover of the envelope. They must see you for you to change their lives. Practically, what this means is your book topic is chosen *for* your ideal reader, not for you. Practically, it's a hard pill to swallow. Realistically, it's the only way.

Only take advice from people who have gotten the result you want multiple times and with consistency. I believe in mentorship. Always have. I've invested in teachers, programs, courses, and mentors since I was very young. The challenge with getting advice on your book is that everyone these days thinks they are an expert. Your VA. Your business coach. Your accountability partner. They will all happily take your money or time and do their best to get you the result you want. The truth is, you should *only* take advice from someone who has gotten the result you want dozens or hundreds of times for someone just like you. Once you find that person, do exactly what they say! Until you have that person – keep inventing your own way, don't listen to people who don't have what you want.

Never ignore advice from people who have gotten the same result you want multiple times and with consistency. I know this is just the other side of the same coin but it's an important distinction. You have to stop listening to people who haven't achieved the outcome you want. But you also *must stop arguing* with people who have consistently gotten the results you want for other people. The reason it worked for other people and not you is because you aren't doing the work required. Many entrepreneurs like to break the rules and create their own systems. You can do that – AFTER your business is up and running. First, get the results you need to sustain yourself and grow your business, then make the tweaks necessary and required. Find someone who consistently gets the results you want and do every single thing they tell you to do – without exception. Do it even if it's uncomfortable – especially if it's uncomfortable! Do it if you have a good list of reasons not to. Do it if it seems completely impossible. Find out. Go all in so you can, as quickly as possible, know if this result is possible for you. If your way was working, you wouldn't have hired someone to help. The right book coach can help you validate your title. If they have gotten the results you want for other clients, trust them.

The world is waiting for your message.

CHAPTER NINE

Is It Worth It to Become a Bestseller?

Becoming a Bestselling author is bullshit.

There! I said it!

It's the truth though. The phrase "bestseller" means so many things that it doesn't really *mean* anything anymore!

It might sound nice tripping off your tongue, but it doesn't say how many books you sold, it doesn't say how much money you made, and, for sure, it doesn't say how many lives you changed.

It's a fairly meaningless credential.

And yet, life is filled with fairly meaningless credentials, right?

I mean, I've had jobs where my boss said to "pick my own title" because it didn't matter to him. So my job title was a fairly meaningless credential.

I've won awards where there was only one person determining the winner and that person happened to like me, so that was a fairly meaningless credential.

I've got 5,000 Facebook friends – I suppose that's a credential – but again, at the end of the day, pretty meaningless. What does it tell you? Not much.

To me, what matters at the end of the day isn't some credential for your resume, it's: Are you making the difference you want with your book?

That's what matters.

All of that being said, on the scale of meaningless credentials, there are some serious upsides to the Amazon Bestseller credential that any author should know about, so I'm going to explain that to you, but before we get to the controversy around Amazon Bestseller status and whether it is, indeed, bullshit or not, I want to give you a little background on other types of bestseller statuses because they muddy the waters of our discussion.

Lots of Types of Bestseller Lists

At any publishing house – and indeed across all books on Amazon – the top 20 percent of books generate about 80 percent of all revenue. At many publishing houses, there are just a small handful of titles that are "paying" for all the other books on the list.

There is an understandable perception that when we talk about bestsellers we are talking about those books that sell the most copies and make the most money. Sort of makes intuitive sense, right?

But "sells the most books" is harder to judge than you might think. For instance, let's say the International Coaching Federation (ICF) does a deal with me to distribute this book to all of its members – that's about 50,000 people. And let's say the goal is to do it in the same month. 50,000 book sales in one month would outsell almost every non-fiction book in America, however, if I go to my local printer and ask him to print 50,000 copies so I get a good price (we can probably get that down to $1 a book so I can give ICF a great deal!), those sales would not be logged or counted anywhere.

I could go through some other services and pay $6 or $8 a book to have the sale counted, but if I did that, the ICF probably wouldn't be able to afford doing the book with me. And there are some other systems that *will* count the sale but they will count it the same as you buying a single copy on Amazon. Meaning 50,000 book sales would count as one sale!

The point of this story is to say there is, sort of oddly, no one way to count book sales. There are lots of lists and they all mean different things which means, essentially, they all mean nothing … sort of!

To add insult to injury, there are bestseller lists (including one you really like) which don't base their decision on the number of books sold at all!

That list is the *New York Times* Bestseller List. The Times' list is what is known as a curated list. What this means is the *New York Times* doesn't look at all book sales when making a decision. In fact, they look at a few book sellers to estimate sales across all book sellers. I can give you a heads-up, the snobs at the *New York Times* aren't big fans of Amazon and they love those stalwart neighborhood Indie bookstores.

I heard a rumor once that if you want to know which stores the *New York Times* curates, find the last president who did a book and look at what stores he went to on his book tour. That will tell you which stores the *New York Times* weighs most heavily.

A lot of people don't like the way the *New York Times* comes up with their list and to quell complaints they used to pretend they had a super-secret, but totally scientific, method for calculating precise sales. And then someone sued them, and they changed their tune. Since the case, the *New York Times* has explained that their list is not "an objective compilation of information but instead was an editorial product."

Okay dudes, we get it.

There are some ways to get onto this list which have been extremely controversial. I won't get into the ins and outs here, but what I will say is this: If you have a good reason to invest between a quarter of a million and a half a million dollars into becoming a *New York Times* bestseller, you can, most likely, get this distinction for yourself.

Most people feel this is a scam, but I know the folks behind these campaigns and they are the least scammy things in the world. What they are is about three years of really, really hard and expensive platform-building work. In other words, you can try to figure out how to build a platform that will set you up to be a *New York Times* bestseller, or you can pay someone who has done it before to help you do it. Either way it's a lot of work, effort, and expense all with the goal of getting 25,000 – 50,000 copies of your book sold, in a relatively small window of time, in a way that is tabulated by the *New York Times* editorial board so you can have a fairly meaningless credential.

To be fair, there are some fantastic reasons to invest hundreds of thousands of dollars in a *New York Times* bestseller campaign. Most of my authors don't have these reasons, but you may.

For instance, one of my clients is generating about $3 million a year with about a 40 percent profit margin. She wants to get her business to about $30 million a year in revenue without compromising that profit margin in the next 5 years. As a part of that effort, she will be acquiring other companies and she knows having *New York Times* bestseller status is going to dramatically change those negotiations. If you are buying or selling your business or other related businesses, being a *New York Times* bestseller can change the valuation of your business or strengthen your negotiating position.

Another client is a European citizen and while he has a seven-figure business in Euros, he is completely unknown in the US. All of his business has been conducted in Italian and he doesn't have any non-Italian speaking clients! He wants to move to the US but his only options are an investor visa, which will require $500,000, and restrict several aspects of his business dealings; or an exceptional person visa, which has no investment requirement or restrictions. A *New York Times* bestseller will almost certainly set him up for the latter visa, which is a much better deal.

Finally, my friend Stephanie is a force of nature. She is one of the world's best business coaches and has used a series of books to grow her business and her bottom line. One day, she was at my house and asked my thoughts about a book – the next day the book was done. I've never met anyone quite like her. That said, self-publishing won't get Stephanie what she truly wants, and frankly, deserves: a national TV show.

Trust me on this one, someday everyone will

know Stephanie and she will be a household name. But a well-timed bestseller campaign can help with that. Steph has a seven-figure business and she invests very wisely in building her brand at a pace that makes sense. She hasn't pulled the trigger yet, but I suspect she will one of these days. If you want to be a household name, have your own TV show, and impact millions, a bestseller campaign can be a part of that effort, but make sure you fund it first. I recommend getting to at least 100,000 fans and followers and at least $1 million in bootstrapped revenue organically before you start thinking about expanding to a broader platform. If the idea of investing $500,000 in your business seems preposterous, it just means you aren't ready yet. That's cool. Be where you are!

There are other lists like the *Wall Street Journal* and the *USA Today* lists that are slightly less ... um ... shall we say elitist? The *USA Today* list does this tricky thing where they combine eBook sales and print book sales which means what you would do to get on that list is slightly different than what you would do to get on the *Wall Street Journal* list which separates eBook and print book sales. But still every list has its own algorithm and there are trade-offs for each.

Don't *Try* to Become a Bestseller

Look, the truth is, this conversation bores the *hell* out of me. Even as I am trying to type this up, my eyelids are getting heavy and my thoughts are distracted by how many more words I have to type before I can reward myself with a piece of dark chocolate. (Yes, I do bribe myself into writing!)

Here's why I'm bored.

Why do you need the *New York Times* or the *Wall Street Journal* or Amazon to get you a credential – meaningless or meaningful – who cares?

How about instead you actually help people, fund your movement, and generate revenue you can use to support your family, your own self-care (which fuels creativity), and build your movement?

There are many books and services and programs that will tell you how to get bestseller status or who to pay to do the heavy-lifting for you – but what is the purpose? Just to stroke your ego? To make your mom proud of you? To finally get acknowledgment from your peeps? Forget it. External validation never works anyway and it's a lot of effort to not make a difference.

If focusing on a bestseller campaign for a day, week, or month of glory is worth it to you, then you are missing the point. I'd want you to use that exact same amount of energy to get a regular flow of fans and customers from your book.

Maybe you are thinking, but Dr. Angela, when I am a *New York Times* bestseller, won't my readers find me and hire me?

Uh, sure, I guess, but what have you given up to get that outcome?

Becoming a *New York Times* bestseller requires you get a traditional publishing deal. As we have already discussed, there is no guarantee you will get a traditional publishing deal.

If you do, it often takes two years or more to get your message out. What is the opportunity cost of those two years for you and for your readers? Plus, a traditional deal requires you to give up a lot. Your intellectual property becomes the product publishers sell to fund their addiction to gambling on books that will fail. Remember 20 percent of books provide 80 percent of gross revenue and just a *few* books on each list will be the difference between profit and loss. Even if you get a traditional publishing deal, you *almost certainly*, will have a book that loses money for the publisher! (Which means they aren't going to give you any more attention than you give to a scratch-off ticket that has been scratched and came up matchless!)

Publishers are obligated to exploit any opportunity for a potential win in terms of book sales, even if it screws you over. There is no increased risk to the publisher once they sign you, so they will do what they can to sell your book, even if it hurts you.

The problem with the publishing industry the way it is currently designed is that no one *in* the industry really knows what it takes to get a bestselling book. "It's an accidental profession, most of the time," said William Strachan, editor-in-chief at Carroll & Graf Publishers. "If you had the key, you'd be very wealthy. Nobody has the key."

Publishers take risks with very little downside to themselves and huge potential downside to you.

Remember my old buddy Ken Chitester from Chapter Four? He had that traditional publishing deal all lined up, but you know what they wanted to hear about? Monica Lewinsky! They knew they could sell *Aboard Air Force One* if Ken tossed a few mile-high blowjobs into the mix. We can't be mad at a publisher for wanting to do this. They have a business to run and the only way they make money is if they sell books. Full stop. But as a communications guy, if Ken wanted to show his next employer how loyal and trustworthy he was, that short-term compromise could have killed his career, even if it left the publisher fat and happy.

Publishers *only* care about selling books.

They don't care about making a permanent difference in people's lives.

They don't care about your movement.

They don't care about bringing hope and healing to the planet.

They don't care about your bottom-line, short- or long-term.

They care about selling books.

So my vote for most authors I work with is to skip the traditional publishing deal – and if you are skipping that deal, then you need to skip almost every bestseller list except one ... Amazon Bestseller status....

GONG!

What Is Amazon Bestseller Status?

Since most lists require a traditional publishing deal and have trade-offs that don't make sense for authors who want to write a book that makes a difference, that leaves us with one final meaningless bestseller credential to consider – Amazon's.

Amazon's rank is at least fair – so let's start there. For every product in the Amazon store, there is a Sales Rank. Once an hour, Amazon tallies sales for each product in their store. At any time, you can go to a specific category you are interested in and look at the products in that category, ranked in order of those that sold most to least in the last hour. This isn't limited to books. You can look for electronic toys for eleven-year-old boys and find what toys have sold the most in the last hour.

Items with the highest sales ranks are "Best-sellers." If you sell the most of all the items in your category, you are a #1 bestseller.

The truth is in any particular hour, even with Amazon's massive number of shoppers, within many existing book categories only 100 or 200 books might sell in that entire category in an hour. The number of books you as an individual author have to sell (*in an hour*) to become a bestseller is very small.

We have authors who have sold fewer than 50 books and become an Amazon bestseller. I know about entire multi-thousand-dollar events where each participant agrees to buy all the other participants' books for $0.99 or download them for free so they can all reach "bestseller" status together. See what I mean? Meaningless credential!

With the books we publish at Difference Press, one of the things we do is celebrate our authors finishing their books with an event we call a Red-Carpet Launch™. We invite their friends and family to virtually attend. During that event (which takes place over the course of an hour), all of our authors become Amazon Bestsellers because so many books are downloaded during the event.

We know it's meaningless.

And yet, it's no extra work, we are already having a party to celebrate their book launch, and to be honest, it is actually kind of fun!

What we have to do to launch the book requires we pick categories and keywords, and so we research which keywords our ideal reader is most likely to search and which categories will be most advantageous to be in. We aren't doing this because we think getting Bestseller status is going to bring some sort of fortune and fame – we are doing it because we know it might help someone who is in need of our help find our book.

I know this is a little contradictory – but it's fun to make a list on a big website with lots of traffic. And while it is largely meaningless, there are some real consequences.

Getting on the list means Amazon is helping to promote your book: They automate advertising for your book on Google and Facebook, they send email to their list to people who have bought similar books, and they feature you at the top of search results for your keywords.

It's nice having a big brand contribute thousands of dollars in free advertising to your efforts to make a difference.

Is it a substitute for understanding how to generate a steady flow of highly targeted leads that will generate tens of thousands of dollars in monthly revenue? No! But it's not something to be ashamed of. It just is what it is.

You can be proud of the fact you sold more books than any other book in your category for an hour or a week or a month or a year. It's a pretty meaningless accomplishment, I agree, but look, it's better than a poke in the eye.

Being an Amazon bestseller generates thousands of dollars in free advertising. It leads to "some number" of buyers finding you who wouldn't have otherwise, and, if you know how to convert book buyers into clients, being an Amazon bestseller will lead to at least a couple new clients and a few thousand dollars in revenue.

It's nothing to retire over, but I am still pretty frickin' thrilled that 100 percent of authors we publish achieve Amazon bestseller status.

At the End of the Day, Just Be Effing Excellent

As I was working on this chapter, I asked myself, "What kinds of bestsellers do I want to help create in my career?" The truth is I *do* care about the hits. Excluding the books in the *Chicken Soup for the Soul* series, these are the ten non-fiction books that have sold the most copies in the last eighty years:

1. Think and Grow Rich by Napoleon Hill - 70 million copies sold
2. Jonathan Livingston Seagull by Richard Bach - 44 million copies sold

3. Your Erroneous Zones by Wayne Dyer - 35 million copies sold
4. You Can Heal Your Life by Louise Hay - 35 million copies sold
5. The Purpose Driven Life by Rick Warren - 30 million copies sold
6. Who Moved My Cheese? by Spencer Johnson - 26 million copies sold
7. The 7 Habits of Highly Effective People by Stephen R. Covey - 25 million copies sold
8. The Celestine Prophecy by James Redfield - 23 million copies sold
9. The Secret by Rhonda Byrne - 20 million copies sold
10. The Power of Positive Thinking by Norman Vincent Peale - 20 million copies sold

Clearly the key is selling 20 million copies. But check this out, here is the same list, ranked by the year the books were released:

1. Think and Grow Rich by Napoleon Hill (1937)
2. The Power of Positive Thinking by Norman Vincent Peale (1952)

3. Jonathan Livingston Seagull by Richard Bach (1970)
4. Your Erroneous Zones by Wayne Dyer (1976)
5. You Can Heal Your Life by Louise Hay (1984)
6. The 7 Habits of Highly Effective People by Stephen R. Covey (1989)
7. The Celestine Prophecy by James Redfield (1993)
8. Who Moved My Cheese? by Spencer Johnson (1998)
9. The Purpose Driven Life by Rick Warren (2002)
10. The Secret by Rhonda Byrne (2006)

It's about two books a decade in my lifetime. There are about 200,000 non-fiction books published each year. That means about one in a million books make this list each decade.

Do I hope your book is that one in a million? Sure! But rather than worry about going for that, let's focus on what we can make actionable – using your book to attract people who you can create permanent change for in a short amount of time. If you do enough of this, you probably will end up with a bestseller and you know what – it will hardly matter because you will have so many more meaningful credentials under your belt to celebrate.

CONCLUSION

We covered a lot of ground in this book. If you have been paying attention, you know exactly what it takes to get a traditional publisher to beg to publish your book. You understand the problem with being needy and chasing this outcome and you understand what it takes to make a huge impact with your message with or without a publishing deal. Ironically, as with so many things in life, what we want most is often available when we want it least.

You know what it takes to separate yourself from all the other experts in the personal development space – which is to crown yourself the queen of one specialty that you can be the best in the world at, and practice hard to stay on top of that mountain before expanding it out.

You learned how the publishing industry is changing and how traditional publishing deals have less value than they once did and how even today, nothing can touch the prestige of a traditional deal that goes well. But I want you to remember, most traditional deals don't go well, and in many ways that's worse than no deal at all.

When you put your hopes and dreams in the hands of someone else, you are almost certain to be disappointed. I mean seriously, when has that worked for you?

"I'll be happy when I win the 'most popular' award or the 'homecoming queen' crown."

"I'll be happy when I meet the right guy."

"I'll be happy when I lose weight."

Nope. Nope. And More Nope.

You will be happy when you take full accountability for each and every feeling you have.

We can't control the circumstances in life, but when we control our thoughts, our feelings follow. And ultimately, it's not a certain outcome we want, it's the *feeling* we think that outcome will give us. And that – choosing how we want to feel – the great news is that that is in our control.

I can't guarantee that you will get publishers begging to work with you, but what I can guarantee is that if you follow the advice in this book and you stop *needing* them to validate you with a contract and instead go after the goal you want for yourself, it won't matter.

The best way to get publishers to beg to represent your book is to build an amazing business with incredible clients, that are begging you to take their money and change their life.

The best way to get publishers begging for your book is to have plenty of money to take care of yourself and your family and plenty left over to grow your movement and your platform with no secret agenda.

The best way to get publishers to beg you to be a part of their movement is to have a powerful movement of your own that they would be proud to be associated with.

We've talked about the importance of betting on yourself – and how you can't expect (or maybe I should say you *shouldn't* expect) a publisher and an agent to place a bet on you if you aren't willing to place a bet on yourself. We have talked about self-publishing and marketing as ways you can begin to invest in yourself to grow your movement.

Have you wondered if going for bestseller status would help you get more traction? If so, I hope my chapter on Bestseller BS was enlightening. I've seen no fewer than 100 articles about the shame of becoming an Amazon bestseller, paying to be a bestseller, not paying for it. I am confident there isn't an argument on this topic I haven't heard, but I haven't heard a single other person mention the one argument I shared in that chapter which is that bestseller status on Amazon is neither the answer to all your entrepreneurial challenges nor is it the root of all evil. It's just a simple technique to optimize the Amazon search engine, and not a whole lot more. Funny how bent out of shape people get over that one. Well, at least now you know!

And in my favorite chapter, we talked about the biggest mistake I see nascent difference-makers make: They confuse "selling" and "installing." Seriously, that chapter alone can be worth millions of dollars for you if you really take that in. You must make something sellable and sell it and the best way to do that is to find a problem you can be the best in the world at solving, and offer to solve it for people in exchange for money – before you create or build anything. If you can't get people to say yes and give you money before you build something, you won't be able to get them to say yes after.

So yes, much like the 615 odd kilometers I covered from Vienna to Belgrade on my trip down the Danube while writing this book, we have covered lots of territory – but I can't leave you without saying one more thing. It's the most important thing in the book, so I hope you will pay attention.

There is a 99.9 percent chance you are going to ignore all the advice in this book – even the advice you agreed with.

There is a 99.9 percent chance you are going to keep doing what you are doing and hope some miracle occurs and you win your scratch-off game of life.

There is a 99.9 percent chance your ego, your fears you aren't good enough, your worries about how other people will perceive you, will stop you from doing what you need to do to make the difference you were born to make.

Marianne Williamson said, "Our deepest fear is not that we are inadequate. Our deepest fear is that we are powerful beyond measure."

And it is that fear – the fear of the brightness of our light – that I see hold most people back from becoming their best and highest self and impacting the planet in the deepest possible way.

But there is a 1 percent of the 1 percent... the 0.1 percent of readers who will know: this is their time. That 0.1 percent will know they may have tried other things for months or years or decades, but that a portal has opened up with this book to finally make the difference they were born to make.

My wish for you is that if these ideas didn't resonate with your heartstrings, that you simply give the book away or leave it on a coffee house end table and never think about it again. But if there is a part of you that knows there is a deep and mystical truth locked in these pages, I hope you will make the decision today to bet on yourself in the biggest, scariest way you can imagine – and a little beyond that.

Maybe you will want my help or maybe you can do this on your own, but either way I want you to know you can do this.

Imagine what you wanted from a publisher when you picked up this book. Maybe you imagined the conversation when the publisher looked in your eyes and said, "This is the book we have been waiting for." Maybe you were excited to have an advance of tens of thousands or even hundreds of thousands of dollars recognizing the wisdom that has come through your struggles. Maybe you were imagining not ever having to worry about doing marketing for your movement because you thought a publisher was coming to save you.

How would those dreams coming true make you feel?

Here's the surprise. You can have those feelings now!

Write yourself an offer letter, give yourself an advance, sweep yourself off your own feet, and become the publisher of your dreams.

ACKNOWLEDGMENTS

One of the rules I have for my authors is that you have to write your book with joy and ease – not because I care if your writing experience is joyful and easy but because the energy that goes into the book is the energy that comes out of it and if we want to bring hope and healing to the planet that same joy and ease must be a fundamental part of the creation process.

I have to thank my husband, my mom and my mother-in-law for joining me on the Danube River Cruise that inspired this book and that led to it being incredibly easy to write with joy! Exploring Eastern Europe with you while I wrote the book made the experience one I will treasure forever. Usually I reward myself for finishing a chapter with an episode of *The Voice*, this time I was rewarded with things like a tour of a Paprika farm or a visit to a thermal bath. I still love *The Voice*, but this was definitely a step up!

During my trip, I shared chapters and got amazing comments of part of my book from hundreds of Facebook friends. *Thank you!* If you aren't following me already please go to www.Facebook.com/alauriam.

While I was on vacation the incredible Author Incubator team was holding down the fort. I am thankful for the efforts of Mila Nedeljkov, Majeed Mogharreban, Ann Alger, Lindsey George Cornwell, Pam Prior, Maggie McReynolds, Esther Goldenberg, Jenn McRobbie, Robin Thompson, Grace Kerina, Olivia Kosciusko Tritschler, Michelle Grierson, Lee Heyward, Cynthia Blair Kane, Ben Wroe, Karen Stultz and Brian DeMocker.

Finally, no author would be complete without readers, for everyone who has shared that my message has given them an aha moment, either through email, FB comments, or Amazon reviews; please know this book would not have happened without you. I would have kept these ideas for our authors and clients and not shared them if it weren't for your begging for more from me. So thank you for your persistence and your belief in me and The Author Incubator message.

Capio Penna!

Seize the Plume!

ABOUT THE AUTHOR

Dr. Angela E. Lauria is the founder of The Author Incubator™ and creator of the Difference Process™ for writing a book that matters. In 2017, The Author Incubator was ranked #285 on the Inc. 500 fastest growing companies and #260 on Entrepreneur Magazine's Entrepreneur 360. Dr. Angela won the 2017 Coach/Mentor of the Year Award and her program, The Author's Way was named Coaching Program of the Year by the Stevie Awards. Dr. Angela was also named, by Entrepreneur Magazine, as one of the top 10 most inspiring entrepreneurs to watch – one of only 2 women on the list.

Dr. Angela hosts ˆPage UPˆ, a podcast which provides inspiration and information for authors who want to leverage a book to reach more people with their message. Helping people free their inner author since 1994, she has helped over 300 authors-in transformation write, publish, and promote their books. Her clients have been seen everywhere from Vanity Fair to O Magazine to the Today Show, and their books have been responsible for over $10 million in cumulative revenue.

She is the author of *The Difference: 10 Steps To Writing A Book That Matters*, *The Incubated Author: 10 Steps to Start a Movement with Your Message*, and *Make 'Em Beg to Be Your Client: The Nonfiction Authors' Guide to Selling, Serving and Funding a Movement*. She lives at The Author Castle in McLean, Virginia, with her husband Paul, her son Jesse, and their Castle cats, Chaos and Princess Feathers McFuzz Bucket.

ABOUT
DIFFERENCE PRESS

Difference Press is the exclusive publishing arm of The Author Incubator, an educational company for entrepreneurs, including life coaches, healers, consultants, and community leaders, looking for a comprehensive solution to get their books written, published, and promoted. Its founder, Dr. Angela Lauria, has been bringing to life the literary ventures of hundreds of authors-in-transformation since 1994.

A boutique-style self-publishing service for clients of The Author Incubator, Difference Press boasts a fair and easy-to-understand profit structure, low-priced author copies, and author-friendly contract terms. Most importantly, all of our #incubatedauthors maintain ownership of their copyright at all times.

Let's Start a Movement with Your Message

In a market where hundreds of thousands of books are published every year and are never heard from again, The Author Incubator is different. Not only do all Difference Press books reach Amazon bestseller status, but all of our authors are actively changing lives and making a difference.

Since launching in 2013, we've served over 500 authors who came to us with an idea for a book and were able to write it and get it self-published in less than 6 months. In addition, more than 100 of those books were picked up by traditional publishers and are now available in book stores. We do this by selecting the highest quality and highest potential applicants for our future programs.

Our program doesn't just teach you how to write a book - our team of coaches, developmental editors, copy editors, art directors, and marketing experts incubate you from book idea to published bestseller, ensuring that the book you create can actually make a difference in the world. Then we give you the training you need to use your book to make the difference in the world, or to create a business out of serving your readers.

Are You Ready to Make a Difference?

You've seen other people make a difference with a book. Now it's your turn. If you are ready to stop watching and start taking massive action, go to http://theauthorincubator.com/apply/.

"Yes, I'm ready!"

OTHER BOOKS BY DR. ANGELA LAURIA

The Difference: 10 Steps to Write a Book that Matters (Released: December 13, 2014)

The Incubated Author: 10 Steps to Start a Movement (Released: January 17, 2016)

Make 'Em Beg to Be Your Client: The Nonfiction Authors' Guide to Selling, Serving and Funding a Movement (Released: March 21, 2018)

OTHER BOOKS BY DIFFERENCE PRESS

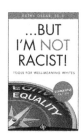

Your Key to the Akashic Records: Fulfill Your Soul's Highest Potential

by Jiayuh Chyan

...But I'm Not Racist!: Tools for Well-Meaning Whites

by Kathy Obear

Who the Fuck Am I To Be a Coach: A Warrior's Guide to Building a Wildly Successful Coaching Business From the Inside Out

by Megan Jo Wilson

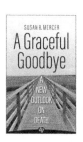

A Graceful Goodvye: A New Outlook on Death

by Susan B. Mercer

Lasting Love At Last: The Gay Guide To Attracting the Relationship of Your Dreams

by Amari Ice

Finding Time to Lead: Seven Practices to Unleash Outrageous Potential

by Leslie Peters

The Magical Business Method: Define Your Stardust, Attract Your Tribe, Make Lots of Money

by Tamara Arnold

THANK YOU

Thanks for taking the time to read *Make 'Em Beg to Publish Your Book*. Many readers discover the fastest path to getting a traditional publisher hot for your book is to have the money to grow your platform and fund your movement. I find the most powerful way to do that is to write a book that creates $250,000 - $300,000 in profit a year so you can afford your own lifestyle and still have money left over to invest in your movement.

If that was the conclusion you reached as well, please enjoy my complimentary Turbo Training. I've created an intense *twenty-minute training on exactly how to write a book that creates $288,000 per year* for readers. You can get it by going to www.QuarterMillionBook.com.

Most books don't generate revenue like this – in fact most generate $250 for the author, not $250,000 – because their authors don't understand the essential components of how to engage readers beyond the page, and how to write a book that becomes a non-stop funnel that creates new clients out of people searching for the problem you solve on Amazon.

In the training, we're going to talk about:

- The numbers behind a book that creates $250,000 in revenue per year
- How to pick the right topic
- How to work with your book's title and sub-title so people find you when they search for the problem you solve
- The right way to structure a "client creation" book
- How to turn readers into clients

This is an essential part of the knowledge I teach my inner circle as I help them get from book idea to published bestseller and a roster full of clients.

Get it as my gift for reading the book at www.QuarterMillionBook.com

Made in the USA
Middletown, DE
08 January 2020